UNIT 3

FORECASTING FINANCIAL PERFORMANCE

Financial Strategy

Prepared for the Course Team by Patricia Swannell
with contributions by Clare Minchington and Graham Francis

The Open
University

BUSINESS
SCHOOL

OPEN UNIVERSITY COURSE TEAM

Core Group

Professor Janette Rutterford, *Production and Presentation Course Team Co-chair and Author*

Bernardo Báitiz-Lazo, *Presentation Course Team Co-chair and Author*

Marcus Davison, *Author*

Graham Francis, *Author*

Carmel de Nahlik

Jan Gadella, *Author*

Margaret Greenwood

Heinz Kassier

Karen Kingsnorth, *Course Manager*

Clare Minchington, *Author*

Pat Sucher, *Author*

Patricia Swannell, *Author*

Richard Wheatcroft, *Author*

External Assessor

Professor Paul Draper, *Walter Scott and Partners Professor of Finance, University of Edinburgh*

Production Team

Sylvan Bentley, *Picture Researcher*

John Bradley, *Design Group Co-ordinator*

Martin Brazier, *Graphic Designer*

Jenny Edwards, *Product Quality Assistant*

Anne Faulkner, *Information Specialist*

John Garne, *Computing Consultant*

Roy Lawrance, *Graphic Artist*

David Libbert, *BBC Series Producer*

Richard Mole, *Director of Production OUBS*

Henry Dougherty, *Editor*

Kathy Reay, *Course Team Assistant*

Linda K. Smith, *Project Controller*

Doreen Tucker, *Compositor*

Steve Wilkinson, *BBC Series Producer*

External Critical Readers

Stephen Abbott

George Buckberry

Linda Cinderey

Roland Davis

Mark Elliott

Angela Garrett

Jane Hughes

Ed Hutt

Rosemary F. Johnson

Geoff Jones

Robin Joy

David Kirk

Archie McArthur

Richard Mischak

Professor Chris Napier

Eugene Power

Manvinder Singh

Tony Whitford

Chris Worthington

The author wishes to thank Christine Villas-Boas for her help with the production of this unit and its associated computer exercises.

The Open University, Walton Hall, Milton Keynes MK7 6AA

First published 1998. Second edition 1999. Third edition 2000. Reprinted 2001, 2002.

Copyright © 1998, 1999, 2000 The Open University

Edited, designed and typeset by The Open University.

Printed in the United Kingdom by The Burlington Press, Foxton, Cambridge CB2 6SW.

ISBN 0 7492 9727 1

Further information on Open University Business School courses may be obtained from the Course Sales Development Centre, The Open University, PO Box 222, Milton Keynes MK7 6YY (Telephone: 01908 653449).

3.3

24943B/b821b2u3i3.3

CONTENTS

1 INTRODUCTION

Unit 3 outlines the process by which the past performance of an organisation (as reflected in the Annual Report and the ratios discussed in Unit 2) can be used to form expectations about its future cash flows. How analysts use projected future cash flows is illustrated by considering three categories of potential stakeholders: trading partners, lenders, and investors.

BOX 1.1   'GOLDEN GURUS' OF FORECASTING

As Mervyn King of the Bank of England observed in a 1997 speech to the London School of Economics, '... forecasting, more than any other discipline brings economics into disrepute. The main reason for this is that forecasts are too often presented as a single number – as point forecasts. And prizes are awarded to those whose forecasts turn out to be correct in a single year, rather than close to the outturn over a number of years. Indeed some newspapers give 'golden guru' awards on an annual basis. This is rather like awarding the Fields Medal for mathematics to the winner of the National Lottery for their understanding of number theory.'

It is a common criticism of corporate forecasting that it is impossible to foretell the future and that the only certainty is that any forecast will be incorrect. The criticism is valid, but it would be wrong to conclude that forecasting is a waste of your time. The techniques described in this unit will not provide you with a crystal ball. Forecasting will, however, give you the means to identify a range of outcomes relevant for the decision to be taken, the means to identify sensitivities and problem areas, and the ability to quantify and evaluate the impact of known threats.

LITZLER

'Let's bury the strategic plan with copies of this week's supermarket tabloids and see which looks sillier in five years.'

To fail to forecast is to make the implicit assumption that everything will continue as it has in the past. This may be a fair assumption in some instances, but a very unwise assumption for most organisations which must respond to (predictable) changes in the economy, sector and technology in which they operate.

Leasing is described in detail in Unit 5.

BOX 1.2   GUINNESS PEAT AVIATION

A very dramatic example of the consequences of the failure to anticipate a predictable change in the sector in which it was operating is provided by Guinness Peat Aviation Group. This Irish aircraft leasing company came very close to collapse in 1994/5. The company had grown rapidly during the boom period of the 1980s, purchasing and then leasing aircraft to many of the world's airlines. GPA had based its business plan and forecasts for the 1990s on the assumption of a continuation of their impressive historic growth rate. Aircraft to cater for the anticipated growth in the business were ordered and commitments to repay both bank and capital market debt were based on escalating revenues.

The demand for air travel is closely linked to the economic cycle and given any airline's very high fixed costs, profits fall dramatically as demand slackens in the economic downturn. Any declines in the fortune of the world's airlines would inevitably be reflected in the fortunes of GPA as one of their suppliers.

In the early 1990s GPA was faced with the prospect of accepting the delivery of aircraft for which they had no end-users, making advanced payment on further aircraft orders, or paying huge cancellation penalties. In addition, GPA faced obligations to repay capital market instruments. The extract from the auditors' report included in Unit 2 reflects this period.

The company's problems were ultimately resolved by a complex financial restructuring which involved the sale of the company's assets, allowing the repayment of debt but diluting the interests of shareholders and imposing widespread management changes.

The lesson to be learned from Guinness Peat Aviation (see Box 1.2), in which both suppliers and investors lost a great deal of money, is that, in the words of a director of the company, 'Trees don't grow to heaven'. The economic cycle includes both growth and recession, so basing business plans on the assumption that the recent past will be repeated is often inappropriate. The impact of the economic cycle *could* and *should* have been anticipated. The implicit assumption that all would continue as it had in the recent past cost the suppliers, investors and senior managers of the company dearly.

Very few of you may be called upon to actually prepare a forecast. However, most of you will be called upon to use or evaluate forecasts prepared by others. Understanding how they are prepared will allow you to assess third party forecasts logically. There are commercial organisations that specialise in forecasting corporate performance and we outline the reports or information that they have designed to meet the needs of trading partners, lenders and investors.

Outline of Unit 3

Section 2 is a general discussion of the purpose and principles of forecasting. Sections 3 to 5 outline techniques that analysts can use to calculate future income statements, cash flows and balance sheets on the basis of the organisation's historical financial ratios combined with an understanding of the economic environment and industrial context of the enterprise together with the strategy being pursued. Sections 6 to 8 look at the application of forecasting techniques to three categories of users who focus on very different time horizons, ranging from the very short perspective of trading partners, through the medium-term perspective of lenders, to the almost infinite time horizon of shareholders. The final three sections also consider forecasts prepared by others that may be available to support these three categories of users.

Objectives of the unit

By the end of this unit, you should be able to:

*   describe the basic techniques of forecasting
*   prepare simple forecasts
*   evaluate and use appropriately forecasts prepared by others.

2 INTRODUCING FORECASTING

Before we consider the process of forecasting financial performance, it is worth asking why we need to anticipate future performance. Though time horizons may differ, most users of accounts are actually interested in the *future* financial situation of a company; historical information is relevant only to the extent that the historical patterns provide a basis for the extension of those patterns to the future.

- Investors, especially when considering investments for which a reliable market price is not available, need to choose and monitor investments and will base their choices on the future cash flows they expect to receive.

- Lenders need to confirm and monitor a borrower's ability to pay interest and repay debt during the years that the debt is outstanding and will focus on expected cash flows during that period.

- Managers of any public or private organisation need to judge the financial strength of existing and potential trading partners during the period when accounts receivable will be outstanding.

- Managers in the public sector may need to prepare and evaluate forecasts to plan budgets, evaluate Private Finance Initiative (PFI) projects and plan or structure privatisation.

- Managers of private sector companies need to prepare information for their stakeholders such as providers of equity, debt and trade credit whose focus will be future performance.

- Employees have a vested interest in the prospect of the continuing financial health of their employer in future years.

PFI is also known as PPP (Public, Private Partnership). PFI is described in Unit 5.

2.1 THE PURPOSE OF THE FORECAST

The key to producing meaningful forecasts is knowing what decisions are to be made on the basis of the analysis. Only when the decision to be supported has been defined can you clarify which business strategy you may assume, the range of relevant outcomes within a given strategy, the time period you should forecast and the specific revenues and expenses you should take into account.

A forecast might reflect any number of business strategies. Most analysts must accept the current strategy being pursued by existing management; trading partners, lenders and small investors normally fall in this category. Other analysts – for example major shareholders or lenders to companies in breach of the terms of their loans – may consider a broader range of strategies which they may be in a position to insist upon.

Given any business strategy, there will be a range of possible outcomes (varying, for instance, according to the economic environment or the response of competitors). The decision to be made will determine what range of possibilities should be considered in detail. In some instances it is sufficient to know the worst possible outcome; in other circumstances you may need to know the full range of possible outcomes and, if possible, to carry out a sensitivity analysis to identify the critical variables before making a decision.

The time period to consider will also be determined by the decision to be made. If you are contemplating a trading relationship, then you may be able to restrict your analysis to a company's immediate prospects, whereas if you are contemplating investing in a company, the long-term prospects are relevant.

The final factor that knowledge of the decision to be taken will clarify is which cash flows should be taken into account. If you are a trading partner you may ignore the returns available to shareholders, at least in the short term. You might consider liquidation values since you would rank near the top in any liquidation. As a shareholder, at the other extreme, you should recognise that other creditors, be they employees, trading partners or lenders, will have prior claims on any cash flows that are generated (or liquidation proceeds that are realised).

Each of these factors (which scenario, which range of outcomes, which horizon and which cash flow) are considered in greater detail in the following sub-sections.

2.2 WHICH SCENARIOS?

There are two aspects that influence the scenarios that should be considered in forecasting the performance of an enterprise. The first is whether you should base the forecast on existing management strategy or whether you should also consider alternative strategies. The second is which range of possible outcomes associated with a given strategy should be explicitly forecast.

The first question you should ask is which management strategies are likely to be pursued. As a trading partner, lender or small investor you cannot influence the management of the company, so your forecast should reflect the strategy of existing management. In certain circumstances, for example as a major shareholder, a member of existing management, or a lender to a company that has broken a **covenant**, you may be in a position to impose new and different management strategies.

As we are anticipating the future, we know that there will be a range of possible outcomes, each associated with a different probability. Not every analyst will be interested in the same range of outcomes. The appropriate range depends on the decision being contemplated. For example, an investor with a residual claim on the company's cash flows might focus on the full range of possible outcomes weighted by the probability of each outcome. Lenders or trading partners, on the other hand, may take a more cautious view: they should ensure that the company can meet their obligations in the event of any adverse conditions that are reasonably likely to occur. They may therefore concentrate on conservative or worst-case scenarios. Realistically, it is also likely that a seller valuing a company will elect to present a more optimistic view of its value than a purchaser during the process of negotiating to a mutually acceptable price.

Often, when forecasting is used to support a specific decision, the most useful scenario that you can choose is one that you believe is quite *unlikely* to occur. If, for example, your loan can be repaid or the purchase price of an acquisition can be justified on the basis of a very conservative or pessimistic forecast, you may feel that you do not need to know how much better the future might actually be, even if you will benefit from a stronger performance.

In the extreme, this means that those providing finance to an organisation in such a way that their obligation would rank highly in the distribution of the proceeds of a liquidation (for example, secured lenders) may simply look at the expected proceeds of a liquidation of the company's assets. They may choose to ignore the prospects of the company's continuing operations, secure in the knowledge that even if the company fails, the outstanding obligation will be met in full.

It can also be very useful to 'work backwards'. You can gain great insight, for example, by calculating the level of sales growth that would be necessary to justify the proposed purchase price of a potential subsidiary. If the required sales level is within your expectations for the company you can move ahead; if it is significantly above your expectations you may conclude that the proposed acquisition is overpriced.

2.3   WHICH HORIZON?

Another factor that will differ from analyst to analyst is the number of years of future cash flow that should be considered. In general, the appropriate horizon will coincide with the period during which the company 'owes' them money – as a trading partner, lender or shareholder. A trading partner will focus on a relatively short horizon, usually less than one year. A lender will focus on a period that matches the life of the existing or proposed debt. An equity investor has a right to, and therefore should focus on, *all* future cash flows. As Roger Beale observes in his cartoon, the time horizon can be a crucial element in reaching a conclusion.

This can mean that users with different horizons may take contrasting views. Trading partners may quite sensibly regard a company as creditworthy, while medium-term lenders who are unable to call for repayment at the first sign of any deterioration are unwilling to lend. In consequence, if you are taking comfort from a third party's assessment of an organisation you should ensure that you are both focusing on the same horizon.

2.4   WHICH CASH FLOWS?

It is important to recognise that most users of forecasts are interested in the *nominal* results of the company as opposed to forecasts in terms of *real* or *constant* currency units. Since a company's future obligations are normally expressed terms of nominal currency units, forecasts are also normally expressed in nominal units. Moreover, the historical ratios on which you base any forecast are in turn based on nominal currency units;

the forecasting process is consequently simplified by expressing it in nominal terms.

Whether you are forecasting on the basis of nominal currency units, or constant currency units, you should be clear about your choice. Some of the reference statistics that you will draw on are expressed in constant currency terms and some in nominal terms. You can move from one to the other by adding or subtracting the inflation element, but you must be careful to be consistent.

See *Vital Statistics*, Section 4.4.2, for how to adjust cash flows for inflation.

The forecast cash flows relevant to a decision depend on the cash flows the decision-maker has a right to. A trading partner should focus on the cash immediately available, while a lender might focus on revenues before any payment is made to shareholders. Shareholders, on the other hand, should focus only on the cash flows that remain after the claims of those providers of capital (such as trade creditors and lenders) who have priority have been met.

2.5 THE APPROACH TO FORECASTING

Throughout the rest of this Unit we will focus on applying forecasting techniques to estimate the value of a company. We have divided the process of forecasting the future performance of a company into four stages:

(i)   Section 3 focuses on the expected level of sales and operating profit in future years. The expectation will reflect external factors such as the general level of economic activity and the behaviour of competitors, as well as internal factors such as management strategy and productive capacity.

(ii) Section 4 considers the calculation of the asset investment which would be required to generate the number of units that our analysis of the market suggests can be sold.

(iii) Section 5 considers how the company chooses to finance the assets that are required.

(iv) Sections 6, 7 and 8 illustrate how future cash flows, reflecting the estimates generated in sections 3, 4 and 5, are used by three different categories of users – trading partners, lenders and investors.

Forecasting is an imprecise art. You will see from the worked example of Blue Circle later in the unit that a large number of assumptions need to be made, some of which are informed and some of which are intended to deal neutrally with areas on which the information available is incomplete. This explains why it is vital to carry out 'common sense' tests. If the forecast breaks a trend, for example if profit has been growing at 5% and the forecast shows 10%, you must be able to identify which assumptions have contributed to this result, otherwise there is a risk that the change is due either to an error or to an unforeseen consequence of a neutral assumption.

The number of assumptions means that, even if they all represent sound estimates of what might be expected to happen, the likelihood is that many of them will turn out to be different. It is often safe to assume that the positive changes are likely to broadly match the negatives. However, sometimes, a few crucial uncertainties alone are capable of drastically upsetting the outcome. If that is suspected, it is important to test one or more assumptions by using sensitivity analysis.

Throughout this unit we apply the techniques to the now familiar company, Blue Circle, in order to illustrate the process. The Activities will be based primarily on the application of these techniques to The Boots Company plc ('Boots').

Activity 2.1 _____

Boots is a corporate case study which will be used in this and later units. Review the company's historical performance as reflected in the OUFS (Appendix 1 and CD-ROM 2, OUFSBOOT.XLS) and read the extracts from the 1997 Annual Report (Appendix 2).

SUMMARY

This section reviewed how the decision to be supported determines the strategies that should be modelled, the outcomes that should be calculated, the horizons that should be adopted, and the cash flows that should be taken into account.

3 SALES AND PROFITABILITY

The first step in the forecasting process is to identify the continuing core operations of the company. Non-core activities, non-operating assets (such as investments) and discontinued businesses have value, but there are no grounds for assuming that they will continue to be held or operated in the future. In consequence, the analysis and forecast ideally look only at the continuing core operation. The value of non-core activities is normally estimated on the basis of their current market value rather than through a detailed estimation of future cash flows.

The starting point for any forecast is the level of sales that we expect the company to achieve through its continuing core activities. Once the level of sales has been determined we can calculate the profit that may be retained and the asset investment (both operating and fixed) that will be needed to manufacture the number of units we expect to sell (or to deliver the level of service that we expect to be demanded). The required asset investment, in conjunction with the expected profitability, will determine how much outside funding will be required for the balance sheet to balance.

For the purposes of Block 2, the term 'sales' should be taken to include revenues or turnover in the service sector where, strictly speaking, goods are not sold.

The sales performance, and the operating profit that the company retains from those sales, will reflect a range of external and internal factors. The *potential* sales and profitability will reflect both the general economic situation and the characteristics of the sector. The *actual* performance will also reflect a range of internal factors determined by the company's management.

The forecasting process starts with an estimate of the expected sales and operating profit, as indicated in Figure 3.1. The forecast of further elements of the income statement can only be completed after the asset investment and the consequent financing need has been estimated. The process of forecasting the remaining elements of the income statement – stage 2 – will be considered in Section 5.3.

Sales
– Cost of goods sold
– Selling and distribution expenses
– Administration expenses

Net operating profit
– Interest expense
+ Interest income
+ Equity income
+ Dividend income

Profit after financial items
+/– Sundry income/expense
+/– Gain/loss on sale of asset
+/– Gain/loss on sale of investment
+/– Exceptional income/expense

Pre-tax profit
– Tax

Net profit after tax
+/– Extraordinary income/expense
– Minority interests
– Dividends

Retained profit/loss for the year

Figure 3.1   Forecasting the income statement – stage 1

3.1 FORECASTING SALES

It is difficult to form a meaningful view of the expected level of sales of an international conglomerate, manufacturing and selling a range of products and services in a number of markets, without considering each of the components of its operations separately. The analytical process is simplified by considering as small and homogeneous a group of products or activities as the data will allow. Larger companies normally report both sales and operating profit by division and/or product and/or geographical region and the analyst must choose which breakdown is most appropriate to use in the process of forecasting. The choice may depend on which breakdown provides the most homogeneous groupings or on the company's stated strategic plans. For example, if the company's strategy is to develop the North American market, a geographical breakdown would be more appropriate, while plans to develop a division spanning several countries would make the divisional breakdown the most appropriate choice.

BOX 3.1   DIVISION? PRODUCT? GEOGRAPHY?

The appropriate choice of 'segments' to use in forecasting is often easier to see in practice than in the abstract. Consider Blue Circle, which reports sales and operating profits on both a divisional and geographical basis.

The pattern of demand and profit for heavy building materials tracks the general level of economic activity but with greater volatility in view of the high fixed costs of cement production. The pattern of demand for the heating and bathroom divisions is also linked to the economic cycle, but with less volatility. This is because demand in the heating and bathroom divisions is maintained during the economic downturn by the need for refurbishment and replacements and dampened in an economic boom by the relatively low barriers to entry, particularly for imports. Consequently, it is easier to anticipate the level of future sales on a divisional basis, since each geographic breakdown includes divisions that respond differently to changes in the level of economic activity.

Remember that when you are using historical ratios you may need to take into account mid-year acquisitions and disposals that distort the underlying pattern. Mid-year acquisitions can make it hard to identify underlying organic growth and distort any ratio which combines income statement and balance sheet figures. If you have several years of historical data you may simply ignore the ratios in the year of the acquisition. Alternatively, you can recalculate ratios on the basis of your estimate of a full year's earnings from the acquired, or disposed, company.

Should you need to refresh your memory, all these ratios are discussed and defined in Unit 2.

As we highlighted above, the historical ratios that form the base for forecasting should include only the company's continuing core activities. In practice, it may be impossible to calculate historical ratios that include only those activities. You should consider the possibility of distortions and weigh the need to make adjustments. Looking at the ratios reported by similar companies involved only in the continuing core businesses can identify appropriate adjustments.

As a background to forecasting the future performance of any company, it is helpful to review the anticipated changes in the general level of economic activity. This provides, at the very least, a reference point and an indication of the phase of the economic cycle. Forecast macro-economic indicators such as **gross national product (GNP)**, **gross domestic product (GDP)** and inflation rates are available from national organisations (such as HM Treasury for the UK) and supra-national organisations (such as the OECD or international banks) and provide a useful starting point.

A company can only grow faster than the economy in general by capturing market share from other companies in the industry or from other sectors of the economy.

This is a reasonable expectation in industries with innovative products (such as mobile phones) but very hard to defend for a mature product in a competitive sector where the rate of growth of the economy probably represents a ceiling to the level of growth. Macro-economic indicators are always available – and useful – but you may find further guidance in sector-specific forecasts published by national statistical offices and trade bodies (for example retail sales). These statistics provide a useful starting point that you can develop with the analysis of other factors.

Having identified the rate of growth of the 'environment' in which the company is operating, you can turn to the company's own past performance. Examining how a company's sales have grown in the past relative to the sector provides a useful base for expected future growth. The rate of growth that the company (or its peers) has achieved in the past often becomes a target for the company's management. Since the environment and management strategy in previous years may have been very different from the environment in the future, however, they should not be given undue weight.

1980·1981·1982·1983·1984·1985·1986·1987·1988·1989

CHIEFS
INDIANS

'This is when we should perhaps have taken warning.'

BOX 3.2 LINEAR PROJECTION – A CAUTIONARY NOTE

The folly of linear projection should not be forgotten. The relatively short (often five-year) history on which a forecast is based is unlikely to reflect the complete economic cycle. Projecting performance in a mechanical way on the basis of only part of the economic cycle will always be misleading when a company's performance is linked to the economic cycle.

Blue Circle provides a good example of a company whose financial performance is linked to the phases of the economic cycle. When demand is strong at the peak of the economic cycle and production is close to full capacity, prices and profit margins are high. The high profits attract additional investment in production capacity by both the existing players and new entrants to the sector. However, it is a long process to build additional capacity and prices can remain high for some time. When the additional capacity comes on stream, the increased supply means that prices and profits tend to fall. This price fall is often amplified because the economic cycle has moved to its downward phase and because several entrants have been attracted by the former high profits. In the trough of the economic cycle, profits may be further depressed by the competition to keep cement kilns fired and avoid the high cost of decommissioning capacity. Prices and profits in the cement sector tend to vary in line with the economic cycle, but with more extreme peaks and troughs.

If the length of the economic cycle is longer than the period over which you have a consistent financial history, you will not see both peak and trough, and you risk projecting only one phase of the cycle. Careful thought is required before you conclude that any past trend (good or bad) will be sustained.

Before concluding that a company's sales growth will match the growth in the economy or sector, it is necessary to consider a few further factors.

First, has the company changed the strategy it pursued during the historical reference period? Chairmen or chief executives often flag changes in strategy in the Annual Report and the press and (where they are believable) these should be taken into account. Such changes may range from changes in pricing policy, to a sales drive in export markets or the introduction of new products.

Secondly, where a company plans a change in strategy, it is wise to consider whether the shift in strategy will bring a response from competitors which would lead you to modify the expected level of sales. For example, would a planned price increase for cement when domestic production was at full capacity bring foreign competition into the market?

Finally, it is also very important to consider whether there are any capacity constraints that will limit the growth in sales. You should ask yourself whether the assumed level of sales can physically be produced. In many industries it is relatively easy to increase output (for example, publishing, where it is easy to increase print runs, or add titles and printing presses). In other industries it may be expensive and time-consuming to build the necessary plant to increase output beyond the full capacity of the existing plant; the cement sector provides a good example of the high cost of increasing capacity by building and keeping fired new kilns.

In services, having access to personnel with the right skills and knowledge base is often a major limitation for growth. Another common constraint is having the capability to co-ordinate a growing number of employees.

There may also be other capacity constraints that will prevent individual companies from realising a level of sales growth equal to the growth of the sector; for example, limited access to scarce resources, such as quotas or prime locations.

3.2 PORTER REVISITED

The Porter 'five forces' model outlined in Unit 2 is a great aid to thinking systematically about the level of potential profits in a sector. The model also provides an ideal structure for checking the logic of a company's strategy. Where the strategy is consistent with the characteristics of the sector, we can expect the strategy to succeed. Where the company's strategy runs against the characteristics of the sector we can reflect our scepticism in our forecast.

BOX 3.3   A VIABLE STRATEGY FOR THE SECTOR?

The strategy pursued by Albert Fisher over the period that we reviewed in Unit 2 provides a good example of a company which sought to follow a strategy that ran against the characteristics and trends in its sector. Albert Fisher's stated objective during the period 1992 to 1996 was to achieve higher margins by moving to higher value-added products. The company was processing unbranded, undifferentiated products for the very large retail supermarkets at a time when the supermarkets' own margins were under pressure because of the emergence of international competition. With hindsight, it is clear that failure of the company's strategy was inevitable.

Porter's later article (1996) on sustainable competitive advantage provides further help in thinking about future profitability. Porter observes that the actual level of profit that a company achieves in a sector depends on the strategy it pursues. Companies often tend to move towards the sector norm (or mean profitability) because they measure themselves against their competitors. A sustainable competitive advantage – that is, performance above the sector norm – will depend on adopting a position that contrasts with that adopted by other players, cannot be easily copied and confers a competitive advantage by lowering costs or allowing a premium to be charged.

Activity 3.1

Boots reports sales on the basis of business segments and geographical segments. Which would you prefer to use as a base for forecasting future performance?

Boots' operations are mainly located in the UK, with UK operations accounting for 95.05% of the sales from continuing operations in 1997.

A single division also dominates sales, with Boots the Chemists accounting for 71.65% of the sales of continuing activities. The group's other consumer goods retailing divisions – Boots Opticians, Halfords, AG Stanley and Do It All – account for a further 21.25%. Boots' consumer goods retailing activities, which are located primarily in the UK, account for a total of 92.90% of the sales from continuing activities.

In the light of the group's concentration of sales in one geographic region, and a single division, you could forecast sales on either basis. However, the overwhelming majority of the group's activities are in the same or related sectors (retailing of consumer goods, retail property and contract manufacturing), so the fortunes of most of the group's divisions are closely linked to the UK economy. Given the group's dominant position in the UK market, it is likely that the opportunity for growth significantly above the level of growth in the UK economy will come from expanding the retail chain in overseas markets where the current market share is very small. However, at the same time, diversifying abroad could reduce their incentives to be more effective in UK retailing.

Forecasting sales on the basis of the geographical breakdown gives you a reasonably homogeneous block of activities and allows you to reflect the stated growth strategy of the group – extending the Boots the Chemists chain internationally or being more cost effective in the UK.

3.3 FORECASTING PROFITS

After assessing the company's future strategy we can turn to the task of forecasting profit margins; for most purposes it is sufficient to forecast operating profit margins. There are circumstances (where there is, say, a major acquisition or a change in business mix) when a detailed forecast of the constituents of operating profit margins (cost of goods sold, administrative expenses, etc.) will give a more meaningful forecast. Whether you are forecasting operating profit margins or their components, it is necessary to review the historical relationship between operating profit (or its components) and sales. The historical pattern of ratios, adjusted for any changes in strategy, provides the starting point for calculating the profits you expect to retain from the anticipated level of sales.

Vital Statistics (Section 3.2) shows you how to determine both arithmetic and geometric averages, and which might be more appropriate.

BOX 3.4   PROJECTIONS

Projecting the pattern of historical ratios is more an art than a science. You normally project ratios forward in one of three ways:

- at the average level recorded during the historical reference period
- maintaining the rate of change, whether improvement or deterioration, established during the reference period
- holding the ratio constant at the most recently recorded level.

If there is no pattern of steady increases or decreases in margins, a forecast on the basis of average levels is appropriate. If there is a pattern of increases or decreases you can continue the trend and maintain the rate of change. If a margin shows an increasing trend you may wish to hold the ratio constant at its most recent level to present a conservative forecast. You should keep in mind that, if a ratio is deteriorating, holding it constant would be 'optimistic' rather than conservative.

If you focus on one company in isolation, it may be very difficult to decide whether there is scope for change. The examination of the performance of peers is a very useful guide as to what changes are possible. A company performing more strongly than its peers may have limited scope for further improvements. A company whose performance is well below that of its peers will face pressure from its shareholders to improve performance and you can anticipate these changes in the forecast.

Margins tend to vary according to the stage of the economic cycle. While there are exceptions, profit margins tend to rise during periods of strong economic growth and shrink during periods of recession. This pattern can be quite dramatic in industries with high fixed costs or high 'operating leverage' such as the hotel sector. The rooms and buildings must be maintained and staffed to a minimum level regardless of the levels of occupancy. When occupancy is low, hotels make losses. As their costs are much the same when occupancy is high, they tend to make very high profit margins at the peak of the economic cycle. General macro-economic forecasts are available to predict the phases of the economic cycle, so profit margin forecasts can reflect this pattern.

A further general factor that you should take into account is the impact of the general environment on the company's pricing policy and the consequent effect on operating profits. If the market for a company's products is growing quickly, even a company operating in a fragmented sector producing undifferentiated products will feel less pressure on pricing and enjoy a relatively high rate of operating profitability. Conversely, if the market is stagnant or growing only slowly, prices are likely to be held down or cut as companies seek to improve their positions at the expense of their competitors.

Profit margins may move from historical levels because of changes in the business mix as different divisions, with different profit margins, grow at different rates. When profit margins and growth rates differ among divisions, and you are not able to forecast by division, the changing balance can be reflected in adjustments to the margins you are forecasting.

A company's selected strategy may also include elements that will cause margins to move from historical levels. If, for example, the strategy is to cut prices or move to higher value-added products, margins will need to be adjusted from the historical levels to reflect these strategic changes.

Finally, it is necessary to consider whether competitors' strategies will have an impact on the company's profit margins. Competitors' strategies may introduce changes to which a company must respond. For example, the entrance of continental European discount supermarket chains into the UK market has forced the established UK supermarkets to change their pricing policy and reduce margins.

BOX 3.5   BLUE CIRCLE ILLUSTRATION

The process of forecasting sales and profitability will be illustrated through a discussion of how a lender contemplating a five-year loan to Blue Circle might approach the task.

Lenders make a relatively modest return on lending money, so they should be very certain that the debt will be repaid. It is appropriate that they base their decision on an anticipated future performance that they are confident will be realised by making fairly conservative assumptions.

As the debt will be repaid within five years, a prospective lender may not look beyond that period.

The performances of the Group's four principal divisions – heavy building materials, heating, bathrooms and property – are linked to the level of economic activity. The divisions, however, are not equally affected by changes in the level of economic activity. The fixed costs in the heavy building materials sector ensure that both sales and profitability will change quite dramatically in response to changes in demand and hence the volume of production. The heating and bathroom sectors typically report a less extreme response to changes in the level of economic activity; this is because fixed costs are lower and they benefit from demand arising from repairs and refurbishment during an economic downturn and face new entrants and imports when economic activity increases. The performance of the property sector, while related to the general level of economic activity, is more significantly affected by the precise location of the property.

In view of the differing responses among the divisions to changes in demand arising from changes in the general level of economic activity, the divisional rather than the geographical breakdown of activities provides the most useful elements for projecting future sales and profitability.

Table 3.1 summarises the sales and profitability of each of the divisions from 1993 to 1997.

The complete five-year analysis of Blue Circle's accounts can be found on CD-ROM 2 in the file OUFSBCIB.XLS.

Table 3.1 Historic divisional sales and operating profit					
	1993	1994	1995	1996	1997
Heavy building materials					
Sales (£m)	826.7	876.4	928.8	966.5	1166.8
Change in sales (%)	20.4	6.01	5.98	4.06	20.72
Operating profit (£m)	98.1	145.2	180.7	178.9	220.4
Operating profit/sales (%)	11.87	16.57	19.46	18.51	18.89
Heating					
Sales (£m)	821.5	823.6	655.0	640.3	575.5
Change in sales (%)	24.9	0.25	(20.47)	(2.24)	(10.12)
Operating profit	64.4	67.1	17.1	35.0	50.0
Operating profit/sales (%)	7.84	8.15	2.61	5.47	8.69
Bathrooms					
Sales (£m)			172.4	175.2	174.0
Change in sales (%)				1.62	(0.68)
Operating profit (£m)			27.0	24.6	24.6
Operating profit/sales (%)			15.66	14.04	14.14
Property					
Sales (£m)	24.1	72.3	17.0	30.8	21.0
Change in sales (%)	24.2	200.00	(76.49)	81.18	(31.82)
Operating profit (£m)	5.1	11.0	3.3	11.9	7.3
Operating profit/sales (%)	21.16	15.21	19.41	38.64	34.76

The heavy building materials division is mainly located in the UK, although there are significant sales in North America; the heating division is mainly located in Europe; the bathrooms and property divisions are mainly located in the UK. This means that the anticipated growth in these regions can be used as a reference point for the growth in each of the divisions. The growth in nominal GDP for these regions for the period 1998–9 as forecast by the OECD is set out in Table 3.2.

The organization for Economic Co-operation and Development (OECD) is based in Paris, France.

The OECD (like most such agencies) does not publish forecasts beyond two years, yet the lender needs to base their judgement on the company's performance over five years. A simple assumption for 2000–2002 is that the modest nominal growth rates forecast for 1999 will be sustained for the rest of the period under consideration. Given that these forecast growth rates are well below average growth rates for both the previous 10 and the previous 20 years, these rates seem appropriately modest.

Table 3.2 Forecast growth in nominal GDP (%)			
Region	1998*	1999*	2000–2002**
European Union	4.9	4.9	4.9
UK	4.6	4.7	4.7
USA	4.6	4.2	4.2

*OECD Economic Outlook, No 62, December 1997

** our forecasts

A lender could reasonably assume that the sales in the heavy building materials division will match the rate of growth in the United Kingdom, its principal market. This implied rate of growth is well below that recorded in previous years. Given that real economic growth is forecast during this period and that a full year's contribution from the St. Mary's Cement acquisition will be included, there is every chance that the forecast level of sales will be achieved.

Both the heating and bathroom divisions have reported declining sales in recent years, and they have responded by closing plants and rationalising their activities. As the company states that the rationalisation programme is complete and, since real growth is expected in all their principal markets, a lender might reasonably assume that the company will match last year's sales in these two divisions in 1998. While this suggests a marked improvement on the previous years' performance, it is a reasonably modest expectation. In 1999 and beyond it is assumed that sales in the heating and bathroom divisions will match the growth in nominal GDP in their principal markets.

Sales in the property division show a very variable pattern of growth, but the strength of the property market in the London area suggests that it is reasonable to expect that the company will match the 1997 sales throughout the period.

These simple assumptions suggest sales figures for 1998 onwards, as shown in Table 3.3 (overleaf).

The net operating profit may now be forecast, based on these projected sales by division and an assumed profit margin for each division. As the sales forecast anticipates modest overall growth in all the company's markets, it is reasonable to assume that profits will match the operating profit margins recorded in the most recent year.

In the case of the heavy building materials division, the 1997 net operating profit margin of 18.89% was below the high recorded in 1995 (19.46%) and well above the low recorded in 1993 (11.87%). Given that real growth is anticipated in this market, maintaining 1997 profit margins seems an appropriate assumption.

In the heating division, the 1997 net operating profit margin was above the level recorded during the previous four years, but growth in the European economy and the company's completed rationalisation programme should allow them to sustain this performance.

The bathroom division's performance in 1997 was roughly in line with that recorded in the two previous years, and suggests an attainable target.

Table 3.3   Forecast sales by division 1998–2002

Division	1997 historic	1998 forecast	1999 forecast	2000 forecast	2001 forecast	2002 forecast
Heavy building materials						
Forecast growth rate (%)		4.6	4.7	4.7	4.7	4.7
Forecast sales (£m)	1166.8	1220.5	1277.8	1337.9	1400.8	1466.6
Heating						
Forecast growth rate (%)		0.0	4.9	4.9	4.9	4.9
Forecast sales (£m)	575.5	575.5	603.7	633.3	664.3	696.9
Bathrooms						
Forecast growth rate (%)		0.0	4.7	4.7	4.7	4.7
Forecast sales (£m)	174.0	174.0	182.2	190.7	199.7	209.1
Property						
Forecast growth rate (%)		0.0	0.0	0.0	0.0	0.0
Forecast sales (£m)	21.0	21.0	21.0	21.0	21.0	21.0
Other						
Forecast growth rate (%)		0.0	0.0	0.0	0.0	0.0
Forecast sales (£m)	1.5	1.5	1.5	1.5	1.5	1.5
Total sales (£m)	**1938.8**	**1992.5**	**2086.2**	**2184.4**	**2287.3**	**2395.1**

The property division showed very strong operating profit margins throughout the last five years. This is potentially the most volatile division. Given that the forecast assumes no growth in the sales of this division, it seems reasonable to expect that they will at least achieve the average margin recorded during the past five years, throughout the next five years.

'Other' activities are relatively small in scale, but have consistently brought losses as they include central administrative activities. It is therefore assumed that while sales in this category remain at 1997 levels throughout the forecast period, operating expenses will continue to increase annually at the rate of growth of nominal GDP in the UK, the location of the company's head office.

Both sales and profits of related companies have been excluded from the forecast.

These assumptions maintain the ratio of net operating profit before exceptional items to sales at close to the 1997 level of approximately 15.0%. This ratio is relatively high when compared to the historic ratio after exceptional items, but as no exceptional items are anticipated, the projected levels may be justified.

Table 3.4   Forecast net operating profit by division 1998–2002

Division	1997 historic	1998 forecast	1999 forecast	2000 forecast	2001 forecast	2002 forecast
Heavy building materials						
Sales (£m)	1166.8	1220.5	1277.8	1337.9	1400.8	1466.6
Net operating profit/sales (%)	18.9	18.9	18.9	18.9	18.9	18.9
Net operating profit (£m)	220.4	230.5	241.4	252.7	264.6	277.0
Heating						
Sales (£m)	575.5	575.5	603.7	633.3	664.3	696.9
Net operating profit/sales (%)	8.7	8.7	8.7	8.7	8.7	8.7
Net operating profit (£m)	50.0	50.0	52.5	55.0	57.7	60.6
Bathrooms						
Sales (£m)	174.0	174.0	182.2	190.7	199.7	209.1
Net operating profit/sales (%)	14.1	14.1	14.1	14.1	14.1	14.1
Net operating profit (£m)	24.6	24.6	25.8	27.0	28.2	29.6
Property						
Sales (£m)	21.0	21.0	21.0	21.0	21.0	21.0
Net Operating Profit/Sales (%)	34.8	25.8	25.8	25.8	25.8	25.8
Net Operating Profit (£m)	7.3	5.4	5.4	5.4	5.4	5.4
Other						
Sales (£m)	1.5	1.5	1.5	1.5	1.5	1.5
Net operating profit/sales (%)	–	–	–	–	–	–
Net operating profit (£m)	(11.2)	(11.7)	(12.3)	(12.8)	(13.4)	(14.1)
Total NOP (£m)	**291.1**	**298.9**	**312.7**	**327.3**	**342.6**	**358.5**

The process of forecasting the level of sales and profits may be summarised as follows:

- Clearly identify the business strategy and the scenario (that is best case, worst case, most likely outcome etc.) appropriate to the analytical task.
- Identify the time period you need to forecast.
- Break the data into as many homogeneous components as the segmental information will allow.
- Consider environmental reference points such as the rate of growth of general economic activity or the rate of growth of the sector and the behaviour of competitors.
- Consider internal factors such as production capacity, stated plans and historical growth rates.
- Adjust historical ratios to reflect only the continuing core business.
- Consider the scope for changes in the historical pattern as the company moves towards the sector average or pursues an alternative strategy.
- Calculate the level of sales that the enterprise can achieve and the proportion that will be retained as operating profit.

Exercise 3.1

Boots' 1998 sales have been forecast on the assumption that the sales growth in each geographical region will match the growth in nominal GDP as forecast by the OECD (see Table 3.5).

Table 3.5	Boots' sales forecast		
Region	1997 Sales £m (historic)	OECD Forecast* GDP Growth (nominal %)	1998 Sales £m (projected)
UK	4395.9	4.6	4598.10
Rest of Europe	126.2	4.9**	132.38
Rest of world	89.8	6.0***	95.19

*OECD Economic Outlook, No. 62, December 1997

** European Union

*** Total OECD

The forecast rate of growth of GDP in the EU is taken as an approximation of the expected rate of growth for the rest of Europe.

Estimate the operating profit you expect the company to achieve in each of these regions. List the factors you have taken into account in making this projection.

SUMMARY

This section has outlined the logic of looking primarily at continuing core activities in preparing any forecast. The advantage of breaking a sales forecast into smaller, homogeneous categories was reviewed. The need to adjust historical data for any distortions arising from mid-year acquisitions or the inclusion of non-core activities was highlighted. The reference point provided by macro-economic data and the importance of considering the impact of the economic cycle on the trend in any historical sequences was discussed. The need to ensure that an appropriate and viable business strategy is reflected in the forecast was considered.

The process of estimating net operating profits on the basis of the projected level of sales was reviewed. The need to ensure that the impact of the economic cycle and business strategy is appropriately reflected in the assumed margins was emphasised.

4 ASSET INVESTMENT

Having estimated the level of sales and operating profit expected in future years, the next task is to calculate the assets which will be needed to manufacture or supply the volume of output implied by the sales forecast.

Operating cash (forecast)	Debt (last year)
Net operating assets (forecast)	Provisions (forecast)
Fixed assets (forecast)	New funding need
Investments (forecast)	Equity (last year)

Figure 4.1   The asset investment: the assets needed to supply the expected level of sales

As you can see from the shaded elements in Figure 4.1, we focus in this section on all those elements of the balance sheet determined by the company's operating decisions.

4.1 NET OPERATING ASSETS

In our discussion of the measures of historical operating efficiency in Unit 2 you saw that the ratio of net operating assets to sales is a key focus for management. There is a clear link between the level of sales and the level of accounts receivable, inventory, prepaid expenses, trade creditors and accrued expenses associated with those sales. As a result we have a means of working back from the forecast level of sales to the level of net operating assets which will be required to support the forecast. As long as there is a stable pattern of net operating assets/sales (which is often the case) you will find that it is easier, and no less accurate, to project the net level of operating assets rather than the individual underlying assets and liabilities. If a company's business mix, strategy or trading environment is changing, however, you may need to take the time to project each underlying operating asset and liability independently.

The level of the ratio of net operating assets/sales during the historical reference period is generally the starting point. As with operating margins, you may choose the average level during the reference period, you may choose to maintain a trend, or you may hold the ratio at its most recent level.

You may wish to modify this simple projection on the basis of the performance of the company's peers. If the company's performance is below the sector norm, but management is good, you may reasonably expect some improvement in the company's future performance. If the company is strong relative to the sector, you should be cautious in assuming further improvements.

As a company's sales grow, it often finds economies of scale associated with net operating assets. For example, a company may need to hold an inventory of spare parts for an item it manufactures but, if one part fails only very occasionally, may find that it needs a single spare on hand whether it makes sales of 100 or 1,000 units. In consequence, a forecast may reasonably anticipate a modest reduction in the ratio of net operating assets/sales as sales grow.

It is also frequently the case that the level of net operating assets/sales varies with the economic cycle. When sales slow in an economic downturn, companies may take a little time to reduce the rate at which goods are manufactured, they may offer longer credit terms to customers to promote sales and they may find their suppliers anxious for prompt payment. All these changes have the effect of increasing the ratio of net operating assets/sales.

Announced or anticipated changes in company strategy (such as a change in business mix requiring a higher level of inventory or lengthening the credit terms offered to customers) may have an impact on the ratio of net operating assets/sales and may be reflected in projections of this ratio. You should also bear in mind that changes in a competitor's strategy may force changes in a company's business. If a competitor offers longer credit terms or a broader colour choice for instance, the new competitive situation should be reflected in the projected ratios.

After examining the historical trend of the ratio of net operating assets/ sales, and adjusting the projections to reflect the influences outlined above, you can calculate the anticipated level of net operating assets for an assumed level of sales. In general it is sufficient to forecast the operating assets on a net basis, but there are situations where it is helpful to look at the individual components (inventory, accounts receivable, prepaid expenses, trade creditors and accrued expenses). If you were preparing a forecast to identify possible cost savings on acquiring a company, or anticipating a change in the trading environment, a change in a company's business mix or a change in a company's strategy, you might forecast the individual components using the 'days' ratios.

Often you see forecasts looking at working capital rather than net operating assets. However, by focusing on working capital, several non-operating items (for example, marketable securities or debt repayable within the year) are included within the forecast. There is no justification for assuming that these non-operating items are in any way related to the level of sales. In consequence, this broad definition may distort the relationship between sales and the operating elements within working capital, making it hard to identify any historical relationship or to justify a relationship to sales in the future.

BOX 4.1   BLUE CIRCLE: NET OPERATING ASSETS

The historical pattern of net operating assets to sales is shown in Table 4.1.

Table 4.1   Historic net operating assets/sales

	1993	1994	1995	1996	1997
Net operating assets/sales (%)	17.92	15.33	17.29	14.71	18.01

The complete five-year analysis of Blue Circle's accounts can be found on CD-ROM 2 in the file OUFSBCIB.XLS.

The most recent year, 1997, is distorted by the acquisition of St Mary's Cement in April 1997. All ratios that combine balance sheet and income statement entries are distorted by the fact that the income statement entries reflect only nine months' contribution from St Mary's Cement, but balance sheet entries include all the subsidiary's year-end assets and liabilities.

The sales projections anticipate only a small change in the mix of activities. The assumptions of modest growth summarised in Table 3.3 imply that the share of the largest and fastest growing division will increase from 60.2% of sales in 1997 to 61.2 % of sales in 2002. This modest change is unlikely to drive a significant change in the pattern of holdings of net operating assets relative to the level of sales. The arithmetical average level of net operating assets/sales recorded in the four years 1993−6 (ignoring the most recent year) provides a reasonable estimate of the net operating assets that would be needed, as in Table 4.2.

Table 4.2   Forecast net operating assets 1998–2002

	1993–1996 average	1998	1999	2000	2001	2002
Net operating assets/sales (%)	16.3	16.3	16.3	16.3	16.3	16.3
Sales (£m)	−	1992.5	2086.2	2184.4	2287.3	2395.1
Net operating assets (£m)	−	324.8	340.1	356.1	372.8	390.4

4.2   CASH

Cash differs from other assets in that it can play two distinct roles within a company. Cash may play a necessary transaction role in the production cycle, as is the case for retailers who need cash in their tills in order to trade. Companies may also hold cash or 'near cash' (marketable securities) as an investment or for other strategic reasons. It is necessary to distinguish between the two uses since the cash used for transactional purposes *must* be held by the company, while the cash held as investment is *optional*. The analyst needs to estimate the required transactional cash balances that constitute the minimum level of cash. This cash requirement is often related to the level of sales. It is an operating asset that must be held just as inventory and accounts receivable must be held. The investment balances, in contrast, may come and go depending on the company's financial circumstances and are usually forecast as residuals arising when the company has excess cash.

Looking at a company's historic ratios of cash/current assets or cash/sales may offer little insight, since the (required) transaction balances and (optional) investment balances of cash cannot be distinguished, no pattern may emerge. In this instance, thinking about how the sector operates and the role that cash plays in the cycle of production can provide the basis of your estimate of the minimum level of cash that will be required in the future.

You should also bear in mind that forecasting models may add any cash not needed to pay dividends or for reinvestment to the assumed minimum cash balances. If cash remains after all assumed payments have been made (that is, there is a 'negative' requirement for new funds) 'surplus' cash may be added to the assumed minimum cash balances to make the balance sheet balance. This investment in excess cash is not likely to emerge in practice, as the cash could be used more efficiently to repay debt or pay additional dividends if it is not needed for investment in the business.

BOX 4.2   BLUE CIRCLE: CASH BALANCES

The forecast of the level of cash in Blue Circle poses a particular challenge. Throughout recent years they have held very significant cash balances, well beyond anything that could be needed for their operations. It is therefore reasonable to conclude that part of the cash balances are held as an investment, and treat them as such. Since cash is not usually a very attractive investment, a conservative forecast might assume that investment cash balances will remain at their 1997 level. The problem is then to identify the cash that is actually needed for operations.

Blue Circle's competitors operate successfully with much smaller cash balances, and can provide a guide to the levels that are an operating requirement for this sector. The strongest UK company with a similar business mix is RMC Group plc. RMC had cash balances of 5.93% of sales in 1997, compared with the 18.75% for Blue Circle (which was the lowest ratio for the past five years!).

Based on the performance of RMC the forecast assumes that cash balances of 5.93% of sales represent an operating requirement and that cash above this level represents an investment.

As is the case with other investments, it is assumed that the cash held as an investment is retained at 1997 levels throughout the forecast period, as shown in Table 4.3.

Table 4.3   Forecast cash balances 1998–2002

	1997 historic	1998	1999	2000	2001	2002
Operating cash & marketable securities/sales (%)	5.93	5.93	5.93	5.93	5.93	5.93
Sales (£m)	1938.8	1992.5	2086.2	2184.4	2287.3	2395.1
Operating cash balances (£m)	114.9	118.2	123.7	129.5	135.6	142.0
Investment cash balances (£m)	248.6	248.6	248.6	248.6	248.6	248.6
Total cash & marketable securities (£m)	363.5	366.8	372.3	378.1	384.2	390.6

4.3 FIXED ASSETS

The pool of fixed assets required to produce a given volume of output can also be estimated by reference to historical patterns, and modified by peer comparisons. Assuming unchanged technologies and a stable business mix, we can make a reasonable estimate of the level of investment in fixed assets necessary to manufacture or supply the number of units of output that the sales forecast implies will be sold.

The relationship between sales and fixed assets is reflected in the net fixed asset turnover ratio defined as sales/(net property, plant and equipment). Given the sales level and the historical level of the ratio, the level of fixed assets required to support a given level of sales can be calculated.

If the company you are analysing holds fixed assets at depreciated historic cost during a period of inflation, the past level of net fixed asset turnover will be too high to be used as a basis for forecasting future fixed assets. Sales will be at current prices while the plant and equipment reflect past prices. If the fixed asset investment is based on a ratio reflecting prices of different vintages, your estimate of the investment needed may be too low. During periods of inflation you may need to look closely at the age of fixed assets and allow for this distortion.

Peer comparisons should be used with particular care when you are forecasting the fixed asset investment. You should carefully consider the possible distortions that may arise when valuation policies differ among peers. For example, some companies may revalue their assets while others hold them at their historic cost. Alternatively, peers may hold assets of different vintages at historic cost.

When forecasting the fixed asset requirement you should also consider the possibility that there is unused production capacity, the possibility that capacity can be increased only in large units, or the possibility that the required fixed assets may not be available at any price (for example a retailer may have no access to further prime retail sites).

BOX 4.3   BLUE CIRCLE: FIXED ASSETS

The projected level of fixed assets must reflect any change in the mix of activities. The sales assumptions that have been made do not anticipate a significant change in the relative importance of the divisions, with the heavy building materials division continuing to dominate. The net property, plant and equipment turnover ratio set out in Table 4.4 shows the historical relationship between the level of investment in fixed assets relative to the level of sales.

Table 4.4   Historic net property, plant and equipment turnover

	1993	1994	1995	1996	1997
Net property, plant and equipment turnover	1.64	1.81	1.78	1.88	1.59

The most recent year's ratio is also distorted by the mid-year acquisition of St. Mary's Cement, so an average for the previous four years provides a reasonable guide to the investment needed to support the projected level of sales (Table 4.5).

Table 4.5   Forecast net property, plant and equipment 1998–2002

	1993–1996 average	1998	1999	2000	2001	2002
Net property, plant and equipment turnover	1.78	1.78	1.78	1.78	1.78	1.78
Sales (£m)	–	1992.5	2086.2	2184.4	2287.3	2395.1
Net property, plant and equipment (£m)	–	1119.4	1172.0	1227.2	1285.0	1345.5

4.4 OTHER ASSETS

There is a range of other assets including intangible assets, goodwill and other long-term assets that are not directly related to the scale of operations. In general, these are not forecast to grow, but assumed to continue at the level reported in the most recent accounts. For the purposes of our simplified balance sheet in Figure 4.1 they have been grouped with investments because they are forecast in the same way.

Investments and non-core activities are also often treated in this way and held at the level reported in the most recent accounts. Alternatively, they may be set to one side while core activities are forecast and a lump sum representing their present market value may then be added to the present value of cash flows calculated in respect of the core activities.

BOX 4.4   BLUE CIRCLE: OTHER ASSETS

The other assets on the Blue Circle balance sheet are tax receivable, other receivables, investments, long-term receivables, investments, long-term tax receivable, and long-term prepaid expenses.

The tax receivable relates for the most part to the payment of Advance Corporation Tax in the UK. This tax required the payment of corporation tax at the time of any dividend payment, but allowed that payment to be set against future corporation tax liabilities. Blue Circle, like many UK companies with operations overseas, did not have UK tax liabilities sufficient to use the total tax prepayment and prepaid balances they had accumulated. The abolition of Advance Corporation Tax was announced in the 1998 budget, so it is assumed that these tax prepayment assets will not continue in the future.

The Annual Report provides little detail regarding the various categories of non-trade receivables, so it is assumed that they will remain at 1997 levels.

Investments, like the investment in cash balances, are assumed to remain at their 1997 levels.

On the basis of the assumptions outlined above, total assets less operating liabilities for the years 1998–2002 can be estimated as in Table 4.6.

Table 4.6   Forecast total assets less operating liabilities 1998–2002

	1998	1999	2000	2001	2002
Minimum cash & marketable securities (£m)	118.2	123.7	129.5	135.6	142.0
Net operating assets (£m)	324.8	340.1	356.1	372.8	390.4
Other current assets (£m)	36.8	36.8	36.8	36.8	36.8
Net property, plant & equipment (£m)	1119.4	1172.0	1227.2	1285.0	1345.5
Investments (£m):					
Cash	248.6	248.6	248.6	248.6	248.6
Other	211.2	211.2	211.2	211.2	211.2
Tax receivable (£m)	0	0	0	0	0
Other long-term receivables (£m)	15.7	15.7	15.7	15.7	15.7
Long-term prepaid expenses (£m)	78.1	78.1	78.1	78.1	78.1
Total assets less operating liabilities (£m)	**2152.7**	**2226.2**	**2303.2**	**2383.9**	**2468.4**

The process of forecasting the asset investment may be summarised as follows:

- Review the levels of net operating assets/sales or days ratios reported by the company and its peers.

- Modify the projected historical pattern of net operating assets/sales to reflect sales growth, the phase of the economic cycle, company strategy (and peer strategy if appropriate), then calculate the net operating assets required to support the forecast level of sales.

- Drawing on your understanding of the sector, and any pattern of historical ratios, calculate the minimum cash balance needed to complete the cycle of production.

- Using historical patterns and peer comparisons as reflected in the net fixed asset turnover ratio, calculate the fixed assets required to produce or support your forecast level of sales.

- Carry forward at book or market value other assets (such as goodwill and investments) which are not related to the cycle of production or not material in size.

Exercise 4.1

Assuming the sales forecast for Boots at the end of Section 2, calculate the level of net operating assets and fixed assets you expect the company will require in 1998.

SUMMARY

This section outlined the process of estimating the asset investment that would be required to manufacture or support a given level of sales. Assets may be divided into three main categories for this purpose: net operating assets, fixed assets and other assets.

Operating assets are most easily forecast net of operating liabilities, reflecting historical patterns, sector norms and company strategies. Operating cash balances, which are also operating assets, should be forecast separately because it is difficult to distinguish between operating cash balances and investment cash balances historically.

Fixed assets should be forecast on the basis of a careful interpretation of historical patterns of fixed asset turnover, tempered by any capacity constraints.

Investments, as they are not related to operations, are generally forecast to remain at the level of the most recent balance sheet. Other assets, which are not material or not related to the core operations, are typically assumed to continue at the level reported in the most recent accounts.

5 THE FINANCIAL STRUCTURE

Now that the pool of assets needed to produce the forecast level of sales has been estimated we should consider the question of how that asset investment will be financed.

- A part of the required finance will come from suppliers and employees as trade creditors and accrued expenses.
- A part may come from the retained earnings from profitable operations.
- A part may come from equity.
- A part may come from debt.

The first element will be determined by your assumptions regarding net operating assets. The second element reflects your assumptions for sales and profitability, the target debt/equity ratio and external variables such as tax and interest rates (to be discussed in Section 5.3). The final element will reflect your assumptions for the future debt/equity ratio.

As Figure 5.1 illustrates, there is a section of the liabilities side of the balance sheet – provisions – that falls outside the definition of operating liabilities, debt and equity. Provisions, also known 'as grey area items', are liabilities such as deferred taxation, pension provisions, minority interests and the like – liabilities with no certain value or due date. In forecasts they are often assumed to continue at the levels recorded in the most recent accounts or they may be explicitly forecast on the basis of historical patterns. Whether they are held constant or forecast to grow, provisions may be represented by a specific currency value that may be deducted from the asset investment. The asset investment *net of provisions and operating liabilities* is then the starting point for the calculation of the debt and equity needed to fund the *net* asset investment. Again, this approach is consistent with the separation of operating and financing decisions since the three categories of liabilities that are deducted from projected total assets – trade creditors, accrued expenses and provisions – reflect operating decisions.

Operating cash (forecast)	Debt (last year)
Net operating assets (forecast)	Provisions (forecast)
Fixed assets (forecast)	**New funding need**
Investments (forecast)	Equity (last year)

Figure 5.1   New funding need

Projected total assets

– Trade creditors

– Accrued expenses

– Provisions

———————————

= Net asset investment

———————————

The mathematics of forecasting requires that you make an assumption about the relative levels of debt and equity in future years (see Figure 5.2). As the cost and tax treatment of debt and equity are different, the relative levels need to be set in order to project the final blocks of the income statement (see Figure 5.3). The assumption that is usually adopted regarding the debt/equity split differs according to the analyst's time horizon.

For example, if the forecasting horizon can be restricted to the short and medium term (as is often the case for trading partners and lenders) it is prudent to assume that no new equity will be invested. It is assumed that debt will be raised to meet the need for new funds and replace any loans and other capital that fall due for repayment during the forecast period. The *implied* assumption is that as the ratio of debt to equity changes it will be acceptable to all parties – that is investors, lenders, suppliers and management. Clearly this is an assumption that can only be accepted for the relatively short periods when the debt/equity ratio is unlikely to change too dramatically.

More on the implications of the debt/equity structure is given in Unit 4.

Analysts (such as investors) assessing a company over the longer term should set a *target* debt/equity structure. This brings an implicit assumption that both lenders and investors will be prepared to provide the funds to meet this target.

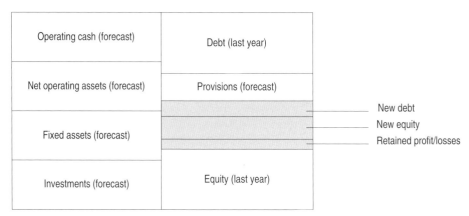

Figure 5.2   The possible sources of new funding

5.1   THE IMPLIED FINANCIAL STRUCTURE

If a forecast is limited to a short- to medium-term horizon, the debt/equity ratio will be *implied* by the profitability assumptions combined with the assumption that new funds will be in the form of debt.

Quasi-equity is a banking term for equity with some characteristics of debt, such as a fixed coupon or a requirement for redemption.

In order to calculate the level of new debt that will be required you need to calculate any repayments relating to existing debt, leases and quasi-equity that must be made during the forecast period. Long-term debt, leases and equity with debt characteristics (such as preference shares or convertible debt) may carry an obligation for repayment during the forecast period. The requirement to repay these instruments is disclosed in the accounts for five years into the future in US and UK accounts and the cash flow required for these obligatory repayments can be very significant. Those users interested in a shorter horizon (for example trading partners or lenders) should consider these very significant obligatory payments relative to the cash available from the company's operating activities. If the cash generated by the company is not sufficient, continued operation depends on the lender's willingness to forgo repayment or the possibility that the finance can be raised from another source. Refinancing can be a particular problem with financial instruments such as publicly listed 'bearer' bonds held by a wide range of unknown investors. It is a brave assumption that the lenders will not insist on repayment or that other lenders will be found: if the existing lenders call for repayment and other lenders cannot be found, the company will go into liquidation.

5.2 THE TARGET FINANCIAL STRUCTURE

As the analyst's horizon lengthens, the assumption that all new funding will be in the form of debt cannot be justified. However, at least one variable must be fixed by assumption so that the forecast of the income statement and the balance sheet can be calculated. The variable that is fixed is normally a target debt/equity ratio. This target debt/equity structure should be based on the funding mix that minimises cost while ensuring that required funds are available when they are needed. The riskier the business in terms of the variability of cash flow, the more the company should fund through equity (see Unit 2, Section 4). The target debt/equity ratio may be inferred by looking at the ratio that management have maintained in the past. Alternatively, consideration of the debt/equity structure of peers can guide you to an appropriate range. The target debt/equity ratio, reflecting both market values and book values, will be discussed in detail in Unit 4.

5.3 THE CHANGE IN THE PROFIT AND LOSS RESERVE

Whether you are forecasting an *implied* debt/equity structure (as is typical for a medium-term horizon) or a *target* debt/equity structure (as is typical for a long-term horizon) you must now return to the income statement. The scale of the investment in assets required to support the forecast level of sales, combined with the existing debt and equity and the assumed level of provisions will determine the new funding need that is required for the balance sheet to balance.

The next phase of the forecasting process is to determine how much of the funding need will be met through debt, how much through equity and how much through the retention of profits (or losses).

New funding need = New debt + New equity + Retained profits (losses)

Sales

– Cost of goods sold
– Selling and distribution expenses
– Administration expenses

Net operating profit

– Interest expense
+ Interest income
+ Equity income
+ Dividend income

Profit after financial items

+/– Sundry income/expense
+/– Gain/loss on sale of asset
+/– Gain/loss on sale of investment
+/– Exceptional income/expense

Pre-tax profit

– Tax

Net profit after tax

+/– Extraordinary income/expense
– Minority interests
– Dividends

Retained profit/loss for the year

Figure 5.3   Forecasting the income statement: Stage 2

An implied financial structure

As we have already mentioned, in the case of the medium-term horizon typical of a provider of debt, it is prudent to assume that there is no new equity and therefore:

New funding need = New debt + New equity
+ Retained profits (losses)

New equity = 0

Therefore:

New funding need = New debt + Retained profits (losses)

In order to determine how the new funding need will be met, it is necessary to complete the income statement and calculate the retained profits (losses).

It is normally sufficient to use a simplified income statement ignoring any exceptional or extraordinary items for forecasting as, by their very nature, exceptional or extraordinary expenses and revenues are not anticipated. Exceptional and extraordinary items may, in practice, be anticipated for the immediate future if the events which cause them have already occurred (for example, the notice of an order for compulsory purchase or announced redundancies arising from the introduction of new technology or working practices), but they can usually be ignored. The equation for retained profits (losses) – the simplified income statement – can therefore be written as:

$$\text{Retained profit (losses)} = (\text{NOP} - \text{Old debt} \times i_{old}$$
$$- \text{New debt} \times i_{new})(1 - T)$$
$$- \text{Minority interests} - \text{Dividends}$$

Where i_{old} = Interest payable on existing debt

i_{new} = Interest payable on new debt

T = Corporate tax rate

The market rate of interest varies constantly and forecasts of expected future levels are available from a variety of sources in most markets, allowing you to estimate the interest payable on any new debt. When the forecast horizon is short, the interest rate a company actually pays may differ from the market rate if the company has committed fixed-rate debt. These fixed interest rates should be reflected in the forecast cost of existing debt. The interest rate applicable to old debt may therefore be different from the interest rate applicable to new debt.

It should also be remembered that many companies will have a seasonal borrowing need and that seasonal debt, while not reflected in the year-end balance sheet, is necessary for the completion of the production cycle and generates interest expense. The identification of a seasonal borrowing requirement may be based on the understanding of the cycle of production or suggested by a historic ratio of interest expense to average debt above market interest rates. So that this necessary expense is included in the forecast, a supplementary seasonal interest expense should be deducted from the cash flows.

Net operating profits, less interest, will be subject to taxation. The applicable tax rate should reflect the historical pattern of the effective tax rate, modified to reflect any changes in the applicable national rates.

Dividend policy may also have a significant impact on external funding through its impact on retained earnings (or losses). While a dividend may legally be suspended, suspension is not a realistic option for many companies. Many pension funds and mutual funds cannot hold shares that fall below their investment standards by failing to pay dividends. Furthermore, many companies have dividend policies (such as annual growth in dividends in cash terms) which are only indirectly related to the level of earnings. This means that the users of accounts with short horizons may correctly regard dividends as a fixed obligation that will be met by the company as a priority. The calculation of dividends on the basis of a fixed amount, or determined by a fixed growth rate, is often the most realistic assumption in the short to medium term. In the longer term, a payout ratio or percentage of profit earned is more appropriate, although it may take many years before the company is forced to adjust its policy to reflect actual profitability. Reviewing the historical pattern of dividends and analysing the commercial position of the company will allow you to make a reasonable assumption about the expected level of dividends.

Minority interests, or that part of the profits of a subsidiary that is attributable to minority shareholders rather than the company, should be deducted to determine funding need. In practice, they are often ignored if they are not material in scale. If they are significant, you should look at the businesses of the subsidiaries in which the minority interest arises, forecasting those businesses in order to accurately project the level of the unowned part of their earnings.

Having made assumptions about dividends, minority interests, the interest rates applicable to both new and existing debt and the corporate tax rate, we are left with a single unknown – new debt. The allocation of new funding need can be calculated by substituting the equation for retained profit (losses) in the equation for new funding need.

In the case of an implied debt structure with its assumption of no new equity the equation becomes:

New funding need = New debt + Retained profit (losses)

Therefore:

New funding need = New debt + (NOP – Old debt $\times$ i_{old}
    – New debt $\times$ i_{new}) (1 – T)
    – Minority interests – Dividends.

New debt is the single unknown, so the equation can be solved and the value of new debt calculated; substituting the value of new debt in the original formula allows you to calculate retained profits (losses).

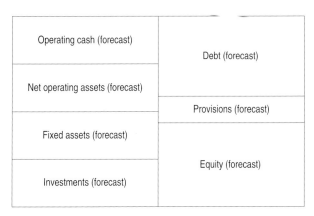

Figure 5.4   The forecast balance sheet

BOX 5.1   BLUE CIRCLE IMPLIED FINANCIAL STRUCTURE

To calculate the new debt and equity that will be needed to finance Blue Circle's projected investment in total assets less operating liabilities (as set out in Table 4.6), it is necessary to forecast the 'grey area' liabilities that are neither debt nor equity. Provisions, deferred taxation and minority interests, which we will call collectively provisions, are sources of funding that are uncertain with respect to the amount and timing of the liability. A conservative lender might make the assumption that this source of finance will not grow, but will remain at 1997 levels throughout the forecast period. The net asset investment may then be calculated as in Table 5.1.

Table 5.1 Forecast net asset investment 1998–2002					
	1998	1999	2000	2001	2002
Total assets less operating liabilities (£m)	2152.7	2226.2	2303.2	2383.9	2468.4
Provisions(£m)	128.0	128.0	128.0	128.0	128.0
Net asset investment (£m)	**2024.7**	**2098.2**	**2175.1**	**2255.9**	**2340.4**

In order to calculate the new funding need on the basis of an implied financial structure, existing committed long-term debt and the previous year's shareholders' equity must be deducted from the net asset investment.

The existing committed long-term debt must be projected for each year of the forecast. Bank loans and overdrafts repayable on demand are not committed funds, so a conservative lender might assume that they must be repaid and replaced with new debt. The committed long-term debt is reduced according to the repayment schedule set out in the 1997 Annual Report. It is assumed that the debt specified as repayable between two and five years is repayable evenly through that period. New funding need may now be calculated as in Table 5.2 (overleaf).

Recall that:

New funding need = New debt + New equity
+ Retained profits (losses)

In the case of an implied debt/equity structure, it is assumed that there is no new equity subscribed, therefore:

New funding need = New debt + Retained profits (losses)

In order to calculate the required new debt, retained profits (losses) must be estimated. The next step is to look again at the income statement and project those factors which determine the level of retained profits (losses) – the interest on existing debt, the tax rate, the minority interest share of earnings, and the dividends payable.

Substituting the components of retained profits (losses):

New funding need = New debt + (NOP − Old debt × i_{old}
− New debt × i_{new})(1 − T)
− Minority interests − Dividends

Table 5.2   Blue Circle – new funding need for 1998

Existing debt repayment schedule

Bank loans and overdrafts repayable on demand (£m):	253.6

Amounts falling due within one year (£m):

Debentures and other loans	5.3
Leasing obligations	0.1

Other borrowings are repayable (£m):

Between one and two years	7.2
Between two and five years	89.8
Beyond five years	252.0

Forecast debt repayment schedule 1998–2002

	1998	1999	2000	2001	2002
Repayment (£m)	5.4	7.2	29.9	29.9	29.9
Existing committed long-term debt (£m)	349.0	341.8	311.9	282.0	252.0

Forecast new funding need 1998

Net asset investment from Table 5.1 (£m)	2024.7
Existing committed long-term debt (£m)	349.0
Previous year's shareholders' equity (£m)	1242.4
New funding need 1998 (£m)	**433.3**

The company pays a range of fixed and floating interest rates on borrowings. The OECD forecast for short-term sterling rates of interest is 7.4% for 1998 and 7.2% for 1999. Allowing for a spread of 0.5%, the company's cost of floating rate debt is projected at 7.9% for 1998 and 7.7% thereafter. Blue Circle has a £156m fixed-rate borrowing at 10.6%, which will be outstanding throughout the forecast period. It is assumed that the existing long-term debt of £349m will bear a weighted interest rate reflecting the interest cost of 10.6% on £156m with the remaining debt of £193m bearing the floating rate of 7.9% for 1998 and 7.7% thereafter. This gives an interest cost of 9.11% for 1998 and 9.00% thereafter.

It is assumed that the company's future corporate tax rate will reflect the national rate of 30.0% applicable from April 1999. It is also assumed that the minority interest share of retained earnings will remain at 1997 levels. Dividends are assumed to grow at 6.4% per annum, the average annual increase over the four years to 1997. Consistent with our assumption of no new equity, it is assumed that there are no further conversions of the convertible preference shares, so the preference dividends remain at the 1997 level of £6.9m.

These assumed values may be substituted in the new funding need equation, and new debt and retained profits (losses) can be calculated:

$$\text{New funding need} = \text{New debt} + (\text{NOP} - \text{Old debt} \times i_{\text{old}}$$
$$- \text{New debt} \times i_{\text{new}})(1 - T)$$
$$- \text{Minority interests} - \text{Dividends}$$

$433.29 = \text{New debt} + (298.88 - 349.0 \times 0.0911 - \text{New debt} \times 0.0790)$
$(1 - 0.30) - 14.00 - 116.60 - 6.90$

$433.29 = \text{New debt} + 209.22 - 22.26 - \text{New debt} \times 0.0553 - 137.50$

383.83 = New debt − New debt × 0.0553

383.83 = New debt (1 − 0.0553)

New debt = 383.83/0.9447

New debt = 406.29

Retained profits (losses) = 433.29 − 406.29 = 27.00

Adding the retained profits for 1998 to the shareholders' equity for the previous year gives us the shareholders' equity for 1998, and the starting point for calculating the new funding need for 1999. Using the assumptions outlined above, the calculations can be repeated to find the new debt and retained profits (losses) for 1999 and the subsequent years of the forecast period, as shown in Table 5.3.

Table 5.3   Forecast new debt and retained profit (losses) 1998–2002

	1998	1999	2000	2001	2002
Total assets less operating liabilities from Table 4.6 (£m)	2152.69	2226.19	2303.19	2383.86	2468.36
Provisions from Table 5.1 (£m)	128.00	128.00	128.00	128.00	128.00
Net asset investment from Table 5.1 (£m)	2024.69	2098.19	2175.19	2255.86	2340.36
Existing committed long-term debt from Table 5.2 (£m)	349.00	341.80	311.90	282.00	252.00
Shareholders' funds, previous year (£m)	1242.40	1269.40	1296.94	1324.04	1350.37
New funding need (£m)	433.29	486.99	566.35	649.82	737.99
Forecast net operating profit from Table 3.4 (£m)	298.88	312.72	327.35	342.59	358.48
Assumed interest rate, old debt (%)	9.11	9.02	9.15	9.30	9.50
Assumed interest rate, new debt (%)	7.90	7.70	7.70	7.70	7.70
Assumed corporate tax rate (%)	30.00	30.00	30.00	30.00	30.00
Assumed minority interest share in retained earnings (£m)	14.00	14.00	14.00	14.00	14.00
Assumed ordinary dividend (£m)	116.60	124.11	132.10	140.61	149.66
Assumed preference dividend (£m)	6.90	6.90	6.90	6.90	6.90
Retained profits (losses) for the year (£m)	27.00	27.54	27.10	26.33	25.21
New debt (£m)	**406.29**	**459.45**	**539.25**	**623.49**	**712.79**

The change in the profit and loss reserve – a target financial structure

In the case of a target debt/equity ratio, new debt is calculated by multiplying the net asset investment by the target debt/equity ratio to give forecast (total) debt and deducting existing debt:

$$\frac{\text{Debt}}{\text{Debt} + \text{Equity}} \text{ (Net asset investment)} = \text{Forecast debt}$$

Forecast debt – Existing debt = New debt

New equity can therefore be calculated as follows:

New funding need = New debt + New equity
+ Retained profit (losses)

Therefore:

New equity = New funding need – New debt
– Retained profit (losses)

and substituting the simplified income statement for retained profit (losses):

New equity = New funding need – New debt – (NOP – Old debt
$\times\ i_{\text{old}}$ – New debt $\times\ i_{\text{new}}$) (1 – T) – Minority interests
– Dividends

Remember:
Projected total assets
– Trade creditors
– Accrued expenses
– Provisions
= Net asset investment

BOX 5.2   BLUE CIRCLE: A TARGET DEBT/EQUITY STRUCTURE

The process of calculating the new funding need is somewhat different when a target debt/equity structure is assumed. The process is illustrated here, based on the assumptions set out in Boxes 3.5, 4.1 to 4.5, and 5.1.

Once the net asset investment has been calculated, total debt and equity are calculated by applying the target debt/equity ratio. In this instance it is assumed that the company maintains the 1997 book value debt/equity ratio of 0.33, as shown in Table 5.4.

Table 5.4   Forecast total debt and equity 1998–2002

	1998	1999	2000	2001	2002
Net asset investment from Table 5.1 (£m)	2024.69	2098.19	2175.19	2255.86	2340.36
Target debt/equity ratio	0.33	0.33	0.33	0.33	0.33
Total debt (£m)	668.15	692.40	717.81	744.43	772.32
Total equity (£m)	1356.54	1405.79	1457.38	1511.43	1568.04

New debt is calculated by deducting existing committed debt from the total debt need (Table 5.5).

Table 5.5   Forecast new debt 1998–2002

	1998	1999	2000	2001	2002
Forecast total debt from Table 5.4 (£m)	668.15	692.40	717.81	744.43	772.32
Existing committed long-term debt from Table 5.2 (£m)	349.00	341.80	311.87	281.93	252.00
New debt (£m)	**319.15**	**350.60**	**405.95**	**462.50**	**520.32**

Total equity is the sum of the previous year's shareholders' funds, the retained profit (losses) for the year and new equity. The proportion of the change in equity met by retained profits (losses) can be calculated on the basis of assumed interest rates, tax rates, minority interests and dividends. The shortfall between the previous year's shareholders' funds and the retained profits (losses) is the new equity that must be subscribed.

> Total equity = Previous year's shareholders' funds
> + Retained profits (losses) + New equity

or

> Total equity = Previous year's shareholders' funds
> + (NOP − Old debt $\times\ i_{old}$ − New debt $\times\ i_{new}$)$(1 - t)$
> − Minority interests − Dividends + New equity

Substituting the values for 1998, the equation can be solved for new equity and retained profits (losses):

> $1356.54 = 1242.40 + (298.88 - 349.00 \times .0911 - 319.15 \times .0790)$
> $(1 - 0.30) - 14.00 - 116.60 - 6.90 +$ New equity
>
> $1356.54 = 1242.40 + 209.22 - 22.26 - 17.65 - 14.00 - 116.60 - 6.90$
> + New equity
>
> $1356.54 = 1274.21 +$ New equity
>
> New equity = 82.33
>
> Retained profits (losses) = 1274.21 − 1242.40 = 31.82

Adding the retained profits (losses) to the shareholders' equity for the previous year gives us the shareholders' equity for 1998 and the starting point for calculating the new equity and retained profits (losses) for 1999, and the subsequent years of the forecast period.

The assumptions and calculations are summarised in Table 5.6.

Table 5.6   Forecast new equity and retained profit (losses) 1998–2002

	1998	1999	2000	2001	2002
Total assets less operating liabilities from Table 4.6 (£m)	2152.69	2226.19	2303.19	2383.86	2468.36
Provisions from Table 5.1 (£m)	128.00	128.00	128.00	128.00	128.00
Net asset investment from Table 5.1 (£m)	2024.69	2098.19	2175.19	2256.86	2340.36
Target debt/equity ratio from Table 5.4	0.33	0.33	0.33	0.33	0.33
Existing committed long-term debt from Table 5.2 (£m)	349.00	341.80	311.87	281.93	252.00
New debt from Table 5.5 (£m)	319.15	350.60	405.95	462.50	520.32
Shareholders' funds, previous year (£m)	1242.40	1356.54	1405.79	1457.38	1511.43

Table 5.6 continued

	1998	1999	2000	2001	2002
Total equity (£m)	1356.54	1405.79	1457.38	1511.43	1568.04
Forecast net operating profit from Table 3.4 (£m)	298.88	312.72	327.35	342.59	358.48
Assumed interest rate, old debt (%)	9.11	9.02	9.15	9.30	9.50
Assumed interest rate, new debt (%)	7.90	7.70	7.70	7.70	7.70
Assumed corporate tax rate (%)	30.00	30.00	30.00	30.00	30.00
Assumed minority interest share in retained earnings (£m)	14.00	14.00	14.00	14.00	14.00
Assumed ordinary dividend (£m)	116.60	124.10	132.00	140.50	149.50
Assumed preference dividend (£m)	6.90	6.90	6.90	6.90	6.90
Retained profits (losses) for the year (£m)	**31.82**	**33.41**	**34.29**	**35.01**	**35.58**
New equity for the year (£m)	**82.33**	**15.84**	**17.30**	**19.03**	**21.04**

The process of forecasting the financial structure may be summarised as follows:

- The operating liabilities (trade creditors and accrued expenses) are part of net operating assets and are usually forecast in conjunction with operating assets as they relate directly to the cycle of production. Asset investment is therefore often forecast net of operating liabilities, as is the case in the diagrams in this unit.

- Provisions may be forecast on the basis of carrying forward the level recorded in the most recent accounts, or on the basis of historical patterns. The value of provisions is then deducted from the required asset investment to give the net asset investment to be funded by debt and equity.

- If you are looking at a short- to medium-term horizon and assuming an *implied* debt/equity structure, the level of debt and similar capital already on the company's books which will remain in future years should be calculated by reference to the repayment schedule, if that information is provided in the company's accounts.

- If you have a long-term horizon you should assume a *target* debt/ equity structure. This should reflect the risk characteristics of the sector and the company's position within the sector.

- The interest rate payable on existing floating-rate debt and new debt should be estimated by reference to forecast market rates. If the company has any fixed-rate debt the weighted interest rate applicable to existing debt should also be calculated.

- The corporate tax rate should be estimated by reference to the company's effective tax rate in the past, modified by any changes to the applicable national rates. Dividends can be assumed on the basis of past policy, modified by strategy statements. Minority interests can be forecast on the basis of historic patterns and an analysis of the businesses that retain the minority shareholding.

- The change in the profit and loss reserve can then be calculated allowing you to determine what new funding will come from new debt, new equity and retained profit (losses).

Activity 5.1

Consider Boots' debt/equity mix in the five years to 1997. You may wish to look at the changes in leverage or gearing and cash flow ratios.

Do you feel that the ratio of debt to equity during the period was appropriate to the business, given the company's strategy?

Boots' debt/equity mix has been very conservative throughout the five years to 1997.

The 1997 special dividend of 44.2p per share (totalling £400.5m), combined with the £300.0m share repurchase demonstrated that the management of the company was aware of how conservative their financial structure had been. The £530.0m dividends payable may be viewed against the £603.0m in marketable securities at the balance sheet date; making this dividend payment required no additional debt.

The effect of the special dividend and share repurchase was to increase the financial risk in the company, with gross gearing rising to 25.22%, leverage rising to 1.15 and total debt/total debt plus equity rising to 0.20. The interest cover (net operating profit/ interest expense ratio of 12.51) and cash flow ratios (operating free cash flow/interest expense of 6.94) suggest that the debt/ equity ratio remained modest.

The company operates in a relatively stable retail area, where it enjoys a dominant position. While there is some inescapable cyclicality in demand, sales are likely to be less volatile than sales in fashion-linked retail activities. On the basis of this observation, you could reasonably expect Boots to have a higher debt/equity ratio than average in the retail sector. In practice, Boots' debt/equity ratio remained low for the sector, suggesting that a further restructuring to increase the group's debt/equity ratio would be appropriate. This could be achieved by borrowing to expand the business or by returning capital to the shareholders. While the group has an impressive record in managing its core Boots the Chemists business, investments outside the core business have been expensive and disappointing. It would therefore seem appropriate to increase the financial risk by returning cash to the shareholders through further special dividends or share repurchases.

Direct comparisons of the debt/equity ratio with other retailers are hampered by different asset valuation policies, but a comparison of fixed charge cover is used within the retail sector to gauge the financial risk. The fixed charge cover for the retail industry is defined as pre-exceptional operating profit plus rent received/ interest expense plus rent paid. Table 5.7 below ranks UK retailers on the basis of this industry specific ratio:

Table 5.7 UK non-food retailers – fixed charge cover (×)	
Arcadia Group	1.4
House of Fraser	1.5
Sears	1.6
W.H. Smith	1.8
Storehouse	2.2
Kingfisher	2.4
Debenhams	3.2
Dixons	3.3
Boots	4.7
Next	5.2
Marks & Spencer	7.2

If you are familiar with UK retailers you will recognise that many of those reporting a lower fixed charge cover might be expected to face more variable demand than Boots. This observation suggests that Boots could justify, and the market would accept, a higher level of financial risk. If you were setting a target debt/equity ratio you could justify a target above the current level and above the industry average, and expect to see shareholder value enhanced by a less conservative financial structure.

More on financial risk in Unit 4.

SUMMARY

This section outlined how the net asset investment is financed. The need for new funds can be met by new debt, new equity or retained profits (losses).

If the forecast is looking at a short- to medium-term horizon, in the absence of other information, it is prudent to assume that no new equity will be subscribed during the period. This *implies* a financial structure, and allows the calculation of the funding that must come in the form of new debt after assessing the expected level of retained profits (losses).

If the forecast is looking at a long-term horizon, a *target* debt/equity structure should be assumed. As the required net asset investment has been determined, this allows the estimation of the new debt required to achieve this ratio. Calculation of the expected level of retained profits (losses) allows the estimation of the new equity that must be subscribed to meet the remaining funding need.

6 ASSESSING TRADING PARTNERS

Now that the mechanics of forecasting have been outlined, we can consider specific forecasts, designed to meet the needs of three different categories of users with contrasting horizons. The first of these are trading partners, who typically have a relatively short time horizon.

Organisations often need to assess potential and monitor existing trading partners with respect to their ability – and willingness – to pay for goods and services. Typically an organisation assessing a trading partner is looking at a transaction that creates a financial obligation of a relatively small amount for a relatively short period of time (30–90 days being common). However, these may combine to form a series of transactions lasting into the medium- to long-term.

When an analyst's time horizon is very short it becomes reasonable to assume that everything will continue as it has in the past. In this instance a trading partner may simply assess a company's recent performance, making the implicit assumption that this will be sufficient to indicate what is likely to happen in the immediate future.

The process of assessing trading partners poses some particular challenges:

- First, the commercial environment often requires that a credit decision be made very quickly.

- Second, as individual transactions are relatively small the potential losses may be less than the cost of assessing and monitoring a trading partner's credit standing.

- Third, independent financial analysis can only be based on published financial information which is unlikely to be available earlier than three months after the balance sheet date; if the justification for looking at the recent past is that it is likely to reflect the immediate future, this delay may be too long.

- Finally, published financial information may simply not be available for privately owned companies.

For these reasons, trading partners may use the services of a **credit reference agency**. These commercial agencies specialise in assessing and monitoring enterprises and advising potential and existing trading partners as to their creditworthiness for relatively small amounts over relatively short periods.

Other credit reference agencies, such as Dun and Bradstreet will follow similar procedures.

The remainder of Section 6 reviews the information provided by Experian, a credit reference agency that specialises in the assessment of trading partners. Section 6.1 reviews the historical financial information and financial ratios that are tracked by the agency. Section 6.2 reviews the index that is used to summarise the creditworthiness of an enterprise, taking into account both financial and non-financial data. Section 6.3 outlines the information monitored by the agency which is not in the public domain.

Credit rating agencies such as Moody's, Standard & Poor's, IBCA and Fitch cater for users with a longer time horizon, such as investors in bonds, other debt and equities. These agencies will be considered briefly in Section 7.

6.1 THE CREDIT REPORT – FINANCIAL RATIOS

The financial information monitored by a credit reference agency includes basic financial information and key financial ratios. Appendix 3 shows the report by Experian on Blue Circle. In addition to providing summary financial information and calculating key ratios, the rating agencies provide peer comparisons with other companies operating in the sector. The 'Industry Report' provided by Experian includes the average values of each financial ratio for the lower, median and upper quartile of companies in the sector, against which the company being rated may be compared, giving a clear picture of how the company ranks within the sector.

Experian's definitions and terminology are not always the same as those used in the OUFS.

This information is available from Experian for more than 500,000 companies in Britain.

BOX 6.1   EXTRACT FROM EXPERIAN INDUSTRY REPORT ON BLUE CIRCLE INDUSTRIES PLC

Industry Ratios

Accounts Ref. Date:	31 December	Last Accounts:	31 December 1996
Last Returns:	15 June 1997		

Quartiles for SIC Code 2410 – structural clay products manufacturing

Comparison based on 208 similar companies

	Company	Lower Quartile	Company	Median Quartile	Company	Upper Quartile	Company
Liquidity ratios							
Current ratio		0.9		1.2	1.7	2.2	
Acid test		0.5		0.8	1.4	1.6	
Stock turnover		3.4		6.0	7.3	11.3	
Credit period (days)		35		52	57	71	
Working capital/sales %		(3.5)		8.2	28.4	28.4	
Creditors/debtors		0.4	0.5	0.6		0.7	
Profitability ratios							
Return on capital %		(1.0)		7.8	17.4	20.2	
Return on assets %		(1.7)		3.6		8.1	12.3
Pre-tax margin %		(4.1)		2.6		10.9	16.4
Return on shareholders' funds %		(1.3)		9.1	24.6	29.6	

	Company	Lower Quartile	Company	Median Quartile	Company	Upper Quartile	Company
Gearing ratios							
Borrowing ratio %		0.0		10.9	43.7	138.3	
Equity gearing %		21.0		49.6	49.9	86.9	
Debt ratio %		0.0		0.0		2.3	22.9
Interest cover		(1.3)		1.2	6.3	16.2	
Productivity ratios							
Sales/tangible assets %		1.1	1.9	3.3		7.1	
Average remuneration/employee £		15,272		17,558		20,448	21,814
Profit/employee £		(344)		3,164		7573	16,053
Sales/employee £		44,684		63,522	97,896	112,732	
Capital employed/employee £		14,578		31,511		65,354	92,404
Tangible assets/employee £		8,139		19,329		45,217	52,130
Total assets/employee		42,754		62,460		114,131	130,871
Remuneration/sales %		14.9	22.3	27.1		39.8	

6.2 THE CREDIT REPORT – RATINGS

As trading partners have a particular need for rapid decisions based on a wide range of current circumstances, credit reference agencies have devised single measures which try to incorporate all the factors which influence creditworthiness. Experian has produced a single indicator, a 'Risk Index' which is a score between 0 and 100. The Risk Index rates companies on the basis of more than 20 factors that are associated with companies which have failed in the past. They include financial elements such as size, shareholders' funds, liquidity and profitability, as well as non-financial elements such as the incidence of County Court judgements and delays in publishing accounts. The Risk Index is regularly updated to reflect any changes in the elements included.

Experian provides the following guide to the interpretation of the Risk Index scores:

BOX 6.2   RISK INDEX

The Risk Index is an analytical tool designed to highlight the strength, performance and ultimately, the creditworthiness of each company in a single score. The score is made up of a number of component parts including the size of the business, the recent trading performance, the strength of the balance sheet and any negative credit information such as County Court judgements.

The resulting Risk Score is expressed on a scale of 0–100, with the highest values attracting the most confidence with regard to credit-based transactions.

The following key can be used as a guide to the Risk scores assigned to each company:

0–10 Companies in this range are regarded as being in the highest risk category. They generally exhibit characteristics similar to those of many other failed companies, e.g. negative capital employed and/or massive trading loss.

11–25 These companies are regarded as being very high risk in that they exhibit similar characteristics to the previous category, although these characteristics tend to be less severe.

26–40 High-risk companies in this category may well have a credit rating but, where such values exist, the rating should be considered as the absolute limit and may require some form of guarantee from the company applying for credit.

41–50 These companies are above average risk and, therefore, assurances in the form of guarantees may be necessary, especially if the credit rating assigned to the company is to be exceeded.

51–60 Companies in this category are regarded as having average risk status and should be treated with a degree of caution.

61–80 These companies have a low risk status and, therefore, there is a high degree of confidence that they will be good for the assigned credit figure.

81–100 These companies have a minimal risk status and, therefore, there is every confidence that they will be good for the assigned credit figure.

In the case of Blue Circle, Experian specified a Risk Index of 84 out of 100 – minimal risk status.

6.3 THE CREDIT REPORT – ADDITIONAL INFORMATION

In addition to the information in the public record summarised in the financial report and the summary index, credit rating agencies may be able to provide timely information on many companies' payment performance. Experian works with a wide range of companies, collecting data on how these companies are being paid by their customers. The experiences of existing trading partners are collated to a give a picture of how a company is currently paying its suppliers. This payment history is summarised to show how quickly companies are paying outstanding invoices relative to their due dates. The company's record in terms of the number of 'days beyond term' (DBT) that payment is made is monitored, as is the industry average for DBT. This database, based on private and current data, provides information that is complementary to, and more current than, the published financial information.

This information is of relevance to potential trading partners who may learn something of a company's *willingness* to pay on time – as opposed to their *ability* to pay on time. Delaying payment is a recognised tool of cash management, but it can also be a threat to small trading partners; it is therefore important to know when, in practice, accounts are settled. This information also provides a potential 'early warning' signal so that any delayed payment can be identified and evaluated before any deterioration is reflected in the published financial statements.

The summary of Blue Circle's payment performance provided by Experian on the basis of the collection information it has gathered is shown in Box 6.3.

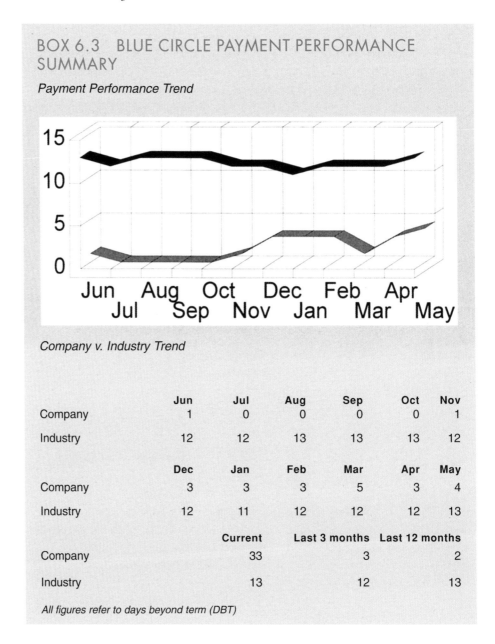

BOX 6.3   BLUE CIRCLE PAYMENT PERFORMANCE SUMMARY

Payment Performance Trend

Company v. Industry Trend

	Jun	Jul	Aug	Sep	Oct	Nov
Company	1	0	0	0	0	1
Industry	12	12	13	13	13	12

	Dec	Jan	Feb	Mar	Apr	May
Company	3	3	3	5	3	4
Industry	12	11	12	12	12	13

	Current	Last 3 months	Last 12 months
Company	33	3	2
Industry	13	12	13

All figures refer to days beyond term (DBT)

Trading partners are interested in the immediate prospects, so the information provided by this payment record adds new information to assist in the judgement about an organisation's immediate prospects.

Activity 6.1

Whether you work in the public or private sector, the organisation that you work for probably has suppliers and customers.

What analysis does your organisation do prior to establishing a trading relationship?

How are existing trading partners monitored?

SUMMARY

The short term nature of the financial commitment of a trading transaction used by trading partners justifies the assumption that all remains as it was in the immediate past. This section summarised the key historical financial ratios that might be monitored by trading partners in order to gauge financial health, either directly, or indirectly through a credit reference agency.

A single 'score' summarising the creditworthiness of a trading partner, combining the information summarised in the financial ratios as well as the factors that are statistically associated with financial health, may be available. Such summary ratings can allow relatively unskilled employees to make appropriate decisions very rapidly, but it should always be remembered that such single metrics do have their limitations.

Information beyond that available in the public domain may be available from credit reference agencies. For example, by purchasing the receivables history of a wide range of organisations, credit reference agencies compile a comprehensive picture of payment practices which, when analysed, can provide both information on a company's payment practices (that is, their willingness as well as their ability to pay) and an early indication of any changes in those practices.

7 FORECASTING DEBT CAPACITY

Banks and other financial institutions lending medium-term debt to an organisation, or trading partners in industries with a long cycle of production (such as contracting engineers), will have a medium-term horizon. Their horizons will coincide with the maturity of the debt or the life of the contract and will usually range from one to five years. They need to know that the cash generated by the company's operations will be sufficient to meet their own and equally ranking obligations arising during the period. This section looks at the approach adopted by such lenders. While perhaps only a small number of you actually work as lending bankers, many – if not most – of you may be involved in borrowing from banks and it will help you to understand the lenders' perspective.

In the same way that trading partners may turn to credit *reference* agencies, lenders may turn to credit *rating* agencies. These agencies provide ratings for traded medium-term financial instruments, but they may also rate a relatively small number of organisations for their creditworthiness in the medium term. Most direct lenders (such as banks) will conduct their own credit assessments, looking to the credit rating agencies for a second or confirming opinion. The agencies play a more significant role for 'indirect' lenders, such as investment and pension funds, that lend to companies by purchasing traded medium-term financial instruments such as bonds. These indirect lenders often have investment criteria that prohibit the holding of financial instruments that do not carry an 'investment grade' rating by a commercial rating agency.

7.1 THE LENDERS' PERSPECTIVE

It is important to understand the lenders' business in order to appreciate their perspective. A lender such as a bank lends money to an organisation in return for a payment of interest, often a market rate such as Base Rate, LIBOR (London interbank offered rate), or EURIBOR (Euro interbank offered rate) plus an additional percentage or 'spread' known as the credit risk premium. The bank must borrow the money it advances from a range of sources, including depositors and the interbank market, and must pay interest to the providers of funds. The bank's net revenue is the difference between what it pays for funds and what lenders, in turn, pay the bank. The difference can be very small (0.125 % or less for a prime borrower in a competitive market!) and is rarely above 3%. With this small interest differential the bank must cover all its direct expenses and overheads, and provide a return to its shareholders. It must be confident that the principal amount of the loan will be repaid if it is to continue operating.

A lending bank is therefore conservative in its forecast of both revenues and expenses. Although it would not be explicitly stated in this way, a lender will probably only look at forecasts that they are 90% certain will be met or exceeded. Lenders may also be concerned with the quality of an organisation's assets available as security against the loan.

7.2 TOTAL DEBT CAPACITY FORECASTS

From this conservative perspective, a lending bank will concentrate their forecast on estimates of the principal sources and uses of cash before the payment of interest and repayment of debt, or **debt service**.

Table 7.1 Total debt capacity forecasts
Net operating profit
+ Depreciation
– Tax
– Expenditure on property, plant and equipment (CAPEX)
+/– Change in net operating assets
+/– Change in minimum cash balances
– After-tax interest on seasonal debt (optional)
– Dividends (optional)
= Cash available to service debt

Contrast this approach with the simplistic interest cover ratio we met in Unit 2.

The elements of the cash flow shown in Table 7.1 should be forecast for each year that the proposed or existing debt is outstanding.

In order to estimate these elements of the cash flow, the lending bank should forecast the principal elements of the income statement and the balance sheet using the techniques discussed in Sections 2 to 4.

Tax may be calculated on the basis of national rates applied to operating profit; the tax payment is often related to the operating profit of the previous year in order to take into account the fact that taxes are payable some time after the year-end. This will be an overestimate of the taxes payable if the company pays tax-deductible interest. The tax saving created by interest is taken into account by calculating any interest deducted *after tax* and using an *after-tax* cost of debt if you are calculating the present value of cash flows available to service debt.

There are some elements included in the cash flow calculation shown in Table 7.1 that may be considered optional. The lending bank must decide whether the borrower's situation is such that they will pay dividends as a priority. Interest on any seasonal debt, that is debt not on the balance sheet at the year-end, is an additional expense that is not related to the debt that *is* included in the year-end balance sheet; the after-tax cost of the seasonal debt should be deducted before determining the cash available to service debt on the balance sheet at the year-end. These estimates or projected revenues and expenses allow us to identify the cash which *could* be available in each future year to service debt.

The annual cash flows may be compared to the cash needed to pay interest or repay existing debt each year. Alternatively, the future annual cash flows may be added together to provide an indication of how much debt the company could borrow, pay interest on and fully repay with the available cash flows. Since you are adding together cash flows that are expected at different points in time, it is necessary to calculate the NPV of this series of future cash flows, rather than simply adding them together.

As the focus is on debt (and we have included a deduction for required dividends to service equity providers in our calculation of available cash flows) the discount rate used for this calculation is the company's borrowing rate, adjusted for corporate tax.

$$\text{Discount Rate} = (\text{Cost of debt})(1 - T)$$

The present value of this series of cash flows may then be compared with the proposed or existing level of debt.

The resulting sum represents the amount of money the enterprise could borrow, pay interest on and fully repay during the period. It is a somewhat crude calculation because it focuses on the amount of debt a company can borrow and fully repay even though we would not expect, or want, to see a debt-free company. The calculation implies that the pattern of available cash – even if it is negative in some years – will be acceptable to lenders. Banks recognise the limitations of the debt capacity calculation and treat debt capacity as a reference point rather than an indicator of the upper limit to debt levels.

BOX 7.1   BLUE CIRCLE: DEBT CAPACITY

Debt capacity is a 'rough and ready' estimate of a company's ability to service debt. It is more meaningful than a simple multiple of current cash flows, but it is often based on fairly crude and conservative simplifying assumptions. This trade-off between accuracy and providing a simple – possibly over-conservative – estimate is justifiable because it is used by lenders who must be certain that cash flows will be available to service their debt in all foreseeable circumstances.

The debt capacity calculation (see Table 7.2) for a company should consider the cash flows that are available to service debt over a period that matches the maturity of the debt that is available to that company. For an established company in a mature and fairly stable industry, such as Blue Circle, this period would be about ten years, while for a software company it would be much shorter, perhaps less than two years. Blue Circle's debt capacity over ten years has been calculated on the basis of the assumptions set out in Sections 3.4 and 4.1. In the previous Blue Circle illustrations included in this unit, the time horizon was limited to five years, to match the life of a proposed loan. As a ten-year horizon is more appropriate when calculating total debt capacity, it is assumed that the cash flows forecast for 2002 will be repeated for each of the years 2003 to 2007.

In addition to those assumptions that have already been outlined, it is necessary to forecast the level of depreciation, since the focus is cash flow rather than earnings. Over the past five years depreciation has represented between 9.73 and 8.74 % of net property, plant and equipment ('PP&E'). As this is a fairly narrow range and no significant change in the business mix is anticipated, it is assumed that the average level of depreciation relative to PP&E over the past five years of 9.34% will continue for the next ten years. The forecast level of depreciation, combined with the change in the level of PP&E forecast in Table 4.5, allows the annual capital expenditure (capex) to be calculated (that is, capex will be the difference between PP&E in the previous year, less depreciation, and PP&E in the current year). Notice that the assumptions that have been made mean that only £2.1m is spent on property, plant and equipment in 1998. The implicit assumption is that reinvestment in depreciating assets necessary to maintain production can be met by selling other assets at book value.

It is also necessary to calculate the taxes that will be paid. The average level of cash taxes relative to operating profit over the past five years is often used as a crude guide to the tax payable in the future. This is indeed a crude assumption since the historic level of cash taxes reflects the tax shelter provided by debt, as well as tax incentives such as accelerated capital allowances and tax prepayments. In the case of Blue Circle's cash taxes prior to 1998, it is particularly misleading since Advance Corporation Tax was abolished in 1998, and the UK corporate tax rate reduced to 30%. For this illustration, it is simply assumed that Blue Circle's taxes paid over the next ten years will fall to 30% of NOP. The tax shelter provided by interest payments is taken into account through the use of interest rates reduced to reflect any tax saving when estimating the debt that the company could borrow and fully repay during the forecast period; tax shelters from accelerated allowances and tax prepayments are ignored.

It is assumed that there are no seasonal borrowings. It is also assumed that dividends are regarded as a priority in this sector and that ordinary dividends will grow at an annual rate of 6.44% (the average annual increase for the previous four years) for the next five years, and stay at a constant level for the final five years. Preference dividends are assumed to continue at 1997 levels. Lenders may choose to make no allowance for dividends when they look at a relatively short forecast horizon, since there is no legal requirement for dividends to be paid.

Table 7.2 Blue Circle debt capacity (£m)						
	1998	1999	2000	2001	2002	2003–7
Net operating profit (Table 3.4)	298.9	312.7	327.3	342.6	358.5	358.5
+ Depreciation	104.5	109.5	114.6	120.0	125.7	125.7
– Taxes	(89.7)	(93.8)	(98.2)	(102.8)	(107.5)	(107.6)
– Expenditure on PP&E (capex) (Table 4.5)	(2.1)	(162.1)	(169.8)	(177.8)	(186.2)	(186.2)
+/– Change in net operating assets (Table 4.6)	24.4	(15.3)	(16.0)	(16.8)	(17.6)	(17.6)
+/– Change in net minimum cash balances (Table 4.6)	(3.3)	(5.6)	(5.8)	(6.1)	(6.4)	(6.4)
– After-tax interest on seasonal debt	0.0	0.0	0.0	0.0	0.0	0.0
– Dividends	(123.5)	(131.0)	(139.0)	(147.5)	(156.6)	(156.6)
Cash available to service debt	**209.3**	**14.4**	**13.1**	**11.6**	**9.9**	**9.9**

The present value of cash available to service debt may be calculated, using the after-tax cost of debt as the discount rate. Table 7.3 sets out how much debt Blue Circle could borrow, pay interest on and fully repay over the ten year forecast period.

Table 7.3   Blue Circle – debt capacity (£m)

Nominal interest rate %	After-tax interest rate % (tax rate 30%)	Debt capacity over 10 years
7.00	4.90	275.13
10.00	7.00	263.70
12.00	8.40	256.75

These totals may then be compared to the actual level of debt on the balance sheet at year-end 1997, £608.0m. Based on these assumptions, the actual level of debt owed by the company is greater than the amount that the company can service and fully repay within ten years. There is little cause for concern, however, when the company's considerable cash balances are taken into account. The company's net debt (debt less cash and marketable securities) is £244.5m, well within the levels that the company could borrow and fully repay on the basis of the conservative cash flow forecast that has been assumed. Moreover, as some of Blue Circle's existing debt is in fact repayable *beyond* the ten-year forecast horizon, there is further capacity to borrow and repay debt *within* that ten-year horizon.

7.3   ADDITIONAL DEBT CAPACITY FORECASTS

The debt capacity calculation makes the implicit assumption that the lenders will accept whatever cash is available to satisfy interest and repayment obligations. In practice, most lenders need a regular pattern of interest and principal repayments in order to meet their own obligations to those who have in turn provided funds to them. The debt capacity calculation can accommodate no cash, or a cash shortfall, before debt service, while this is not likely to be accepted by lenders in practice.

A refinement of the simple debt capacity calculation improves the focus on the required pattern of debt repayment. Additional debt capacity looks at the cash available to service new debt *after* the company has made the contractual payments associated with existing debt (Table 7.4).

Table 7.4   Additional debt capacity forecasts

Net operating profit

+ Depreciation

– Taxes

– Expenditure on PP&E (CAPEX)

+/– Change in net operating assets

+/– Change in minimum cash balances

– After-tax interest on seasonal debt (optional)

– Dividends (optional)

= Cash available to service debt

– Current portion of long-term debt and leases

– After-tax interest on existing debt

= Cash available to service new debt

The tax saving arising from interest on the existing debt can be calculated by multiplying the interest on existing debt by a factor equal to one minus the tax rate. The tax saving or shield created by the interest is thus included as a reduction to the cash interest expense.

This calculation is often more useful. As well as highlighting the annual pattern of cash inflows and outflows, it allows you to take into account the fact that some existing debt will not need to be repaid during the forecast period and/or may carry a rate of interest significantly above or below the current market rate that would be applied to any additional or new debt.

7.4 CREDIT RATING AGENCIES

Credit rating agencies, of which the best known are Moody's and Standard & Poor's, rate traded medium-term financial instruments such as bonds on a simple scale indicating the level of risk of the financial instrument. The definitions reflected in the slightly different bond rating scales used by both agencies are included as Appendix 4.

Credit rating agencies rate companies (as against financial instruments) less frequently. It is important to recognise that the ratings *generally* relate to a specific financial instrument and therefore reflect a specific horizon, jurisdiction and legal structure. Using the rating on a specific financial instrument (which may, for example, be secured on assets) to draw more general conclusions may not be valid.

Our discussion of forecasting illustrates that any forecast will reflect a series of judgements and assumptions. No forecaster, including the credit rating agencies, can always make the 'right' judgements and assumptions. Credit rating agencies make a sophisticated assessment based on comprehensive and current information and therefore provide a valuable confirmation of your own assessment. As lenders in East Asia were shown during the 1997/98 downturn, credit rating agencies are not, and cannot be, infallible (see Box 7.2).

BOX 7.2 CREDIT AGENCY ADMITS IT FAILED TO PREDICT ASIA WOES

Fitch IBCA, Europe's largest credit rating agency, yesterday admitted that it and its rivals, Standard & Poor's and Moody's Investors Service of the US, had largely failed to predict the recent turmoil in Asia.

The admission, accompanied by an attack on the International Monetary Fund for its allegedly poor forecasting record in Asia, followed widespread criticism of the three big agencies over their handling of the Asian upheavals.

The agencies came in for fierce criticism for their treatment of South Korea. The country was rated at the same level as Italy and Sweden as recently as last October but has since been downgraded to junk bond status.

'There were no early warnings about Korea from us or, to the best of our knowledge, from other market participants,' said Fitch IBCA.

In contrast, both S&P's and Moody's have sought to defend their recent record in Asia.

Fitch IBCA, the product of a merger last year between London-based IBCA and Fitch Investors Service, the New York-based agency, admitted the moves to downgrade Korea were 'the most dramatic instances of sovereign rating downgrades in the history of sovereign ratings'.

The agency added: 'Although the facts (regarding Korea) did change, and therefore did justify some downgrading, the extent of the rating actions is too significant to attribute solely to changed circumstances.' The agency said it and its competitors had underestimated the spread of 'market contagion' in Asia. It had also failed to appreciate fully the impact that high levels of external private sector debt would have on the credit-worthiness of sovereign borrowers.

In addition, both the agencies and the IMF had understated the impact that high levels of short-term debt could have on the official reserves of South Korea and other Asian economies. Fitch IBCA claimed the IMF persisted in what it called this 'incorrect practice'.

In the case of Korea, Fitch IBCA said it had been lulled into a false sense of security by the fact that the country had a low overall debt burden.

'We used to think that a high proportion of short-term debt was a worry only with highly indebted sovereigns,' said the agency. 'We were wrong.'

Fitch IBCA and its competitors had also placed too much faith in the capabilities of Asian governments to take sensible decisions, it said.

'We overestimated the sophistication of Asian policy makers, who have proved good fair weather navigators but very poor sailors in a storm.' The role of the ratings agencies is critical because many leading US and European investors are debarred from investing in countries or companies that are not given agency investment grade ratings.

Critics say this gives the credit rating agencies a disproportionate influence.

Financial Times *14 January 1998*

Exercise 7.1

Boots 1997 Annual Report gives the following debt details at year-end:

Borrowings	£m
Bank loans and overdrafts repayable on demand	112.9
Other bank loans and overdrafts	155.5
Variable rate notes	16.1
10.125% bond 2017	97.4
Net liability under currency swaps	7.0
Obligations under finance leases	15.5
Repayments fall due as follows	**£m**
Within one year:	
Bank loans and overdrafts	114.2
Other borrowings	53.7
After more than one year:	
Within one to two years	35.3
Within two to five years	105.6
After five years	95.6

Estimate the cash payments that must be made in respect of this debt in each of the next five years.

Year	1998 £m	1999 £m	2000 £m	2001 £m	2002 £m
Loan repayment					
Interest on repayment					
Interest on principal					

The OECD Economic Outlook, No.62, Dec. 1997, forecast short-term sterling rates of interest (3 month LIBOR) at 7.4% for 1998 and 7.2% for 1999.

SUMMARY

This section reviewed the approach adopted by financial institutions lending money to a company in the medium term. As lenders typically earn a small margin over their costs and have no right to any further remuneration regardless of how strong the borrower's performance may be, it is appropriate that they adopt a conservative perspective.

The cash flows that lenders can call upon to service debt can be approached in two different ways. Lenders can look at the cash available to service *all* debt over a period or they can look at the cash available to service *new* or *additional* debt.

The year-on-year cash flows, whether for total debt capacity or additional debt capacity, can be summarised in a single value by discounting the cash flows to a present value. The appropriate discount rate is the organisation's cost of debt after tax.

There are certain cash flows such as dividends that a lender may consider to be a practical priority even though they are not a legal priority. Interest on seasonal debt is another demand on cash that should be explicitly forecast since the debt capacity calculation looks only at the debt on the balance sheet at the year-end.

8 COMPANY VALUATIONS

The group that should take into account a company's performance over the longest period is its shareholders, existing and potential. Shareholders have a residual claim on the company's earnings to the end of time. There is a range of earnings, cash flow and asset-based techniques that can be used to express the value of an organisation, and many of these are discussed in Unit 6. This unit will consider only discounted cash flow (DCF) valuation techniques, as they are generally accepted to provide the most practical and meaningful techniques for establishing the value of a company, as well as providing an understanding of the forces that determine that value (Sloan, 1996). However, the DCF valuation techniques introduced in this section, and explored in greater detail in Units 4 and 6, are not only of interest to shareholders. Where maximising shareholder value is the implicit or explicit goal of a company, managers should monitor, and manage, the value of their enterprise as the ultimate measure of their performance.

A shareholder has a residual right to all future cash flows. As a practical matter, it is onerous to calculate explicit forecasts into the distant future, and in view of the time value of money, distant cash flows will have a limited impact on a company's present value. In consequence, the valuation of a company's future cash flows is usually calculated over two distinct time periods:

> Company value = Present value of cash flows during an explicit forecast period + Present value of cash flows following an explicit forecast period

The techniques used to forecast cash flows during the explicit forecast period are similar to those discussed in Sections 2 to 4, while further simplifying assumptions and mathematical techniques are used to determine the values of cash flows following the explicit forecast period. An explicit forecast of about ten years (designed to cover a complete economic cycle) is common. The techniques for calculating the value of cash flows beyond the explicit forecast period, also known as the **continuing** or **residual value**, are discussed in detail in Unit 6.

In this section we will look at the process of projecting the future nominal free cash flows that can be used to establish the value of a company during the explicit forecast period. (Unit 4 considers the cost of capital that allows the calculation of the present value of these cash flows. Unit 6 looks at how the cash flow projections and cost of capital can be combined with techniques for estimating residual value to provide an overall measure of enterprise value.)

8.1   THE INVESTORS' PERSPECTIVE

When you are forecasting it is important to recognise that, in contrast to trading partners and lenders, shareholders may have the ability to influence a company's business strategy. Inevitably, when forecasting as a trading partner, as a lender or as a small investor, you should forecast a company's future cash flows on the basis of the management's existing or stated strategy. A major shareholder has the power to influence, or indeed impose a strategy, and may therefore forecast future cash flows on the basis of a 'new' business strategy. The valuation of a company 'as is' can be very different from its value on the basis of an altered strategy reflecting, for example, greater insight into markets, synergies with other businesses owned by the investor, different management styles, etc. If you are forecasting the future cash flows available to a major shareholder you can legitimately consider a wider range of possible scenarios than an analyst who must accept the strategy 'as is'.

The range of outcomes that any potential investor, small or large, should consider is usually broader than that considered by other analysts. Since shareholders have a residual right to a company's earnings, they have an interest in a full range of possible outcomes, both good and bad. They will generally calculate an array of possible outcomes that represent the worst case, the most likely case, and the best case.

Forecasting an array of outcomes relating to a specific business strategy is often more meaningful than forecasting a single statistically 'most likely' case on the basis of weighting alternative outcomes by the probability of their occurrence. To take an extreme example, consider a pharmaceutical company awaiting the outcome of a drug trial and with a 50% chance of regulatory approval. If the drug is approved, the company's prospects for growth and profitability are outstanding; if the drug fails to win approval the company will go out of business. Calculating the weighted average of these two outcomes might show a scenario of moderate growth, which though statistically 'most likely', reveals little about the cash flows that will occur in the future.

It is often the case that potential shareholders 'work backwards' in preparing a valuation. Since they know, or can estimate, what they will need to pay to gain the right to a future income stream (for example, the market price of the shares or an agreed selling price of a subsidiary), they can calculate the level of sales and profitability justifying that purchase price. If they feel confident that the performance needed to justify the purchase price can be achieved, they need not calculate in detail the potential upside gains.

The forecast of free cash flow is useful to investors because it distils the value of the business. A business that is capable of generating a certain amount of cash can be financed in a number of ways. A fairly wide range of financial structures will yield a company of roughly the same total value – any impact of the funding structure within a normal range is small compared with the uncertainty in the free cash flow valuation itself. Producing a realistic forecast of the balance sheet and income statement from the free cash flow forecast is often difficult. This is because mechanical forecasting assumptions, such as holding the ratio of debt to equity constant, cannot capture the subtle interplay of the factors that influence actual funding decisions. However, investors do have legitimate reasons for wanting to see projections of balance sheets and income statements, for example:

- to highlight unforeseen consequences of underlying assumptions
- to verify that the formal accounts will not provide a constraint on dividend distribution
- to verify that legal requirements, such as minimum reserves, can be met
- to estimate the effect of consolidation on the investor's accounts.

8.2   CONSISTENT ASSUMPTIONS

With any forecasting exercise, the assumptions underlying the forecast cash flows should be consistent with each other and the business scenario that you are presenting. In valuing a company on the basis of discounted cash flows, you should *also* ensure that the discount rate is calculated in a manner that is consistent with the definitions of the cash flows to be discounted.

The generally adopted valuation approach starts with the calculation of the total nominal free cash flow generated by the enterprise for all providers of funds, whether debt or equity. These future cash flows should therefore be brought to a single net present value by a discount rate that reflects the nominal cost of all sources of capital, with the return required by each provider of capital weighted by their relative contribution to the company's total capital. Typically, the free cash flows are calculated after tax. This means that calculating the after-tax cost of that source of finance should reflect any tax benefit arising from the chosen source of finance (such as the use of tax-deductible debt).

The nominal discount rate used should reflect the same inflation assumptions embedded in the cash flow forecasts. See *Vital Statistics*, Section 4.4.2.

For the purpose of this unit it is sufficient that you recognise that in order to be consistent with the generally accepted approach to determining the 'weighted average cost of capital', you should forecast after-tax cash flows as if the enterprise had no debt.

The weighted average cost of capital, or WACC, the subject of much academic debate, is covered in detail in Unit 4.

This approach also has the advantage of separating the analysis of the operations from the analysis of the financing of those operations.

Theoretically, it is equally valid to choose a different set of assumptions, for example valuing the company on the basis of real instead of nominal cash flows. The generally adopted approach outlined in this unit and elaborated in Units 4 and 6 represents one practical set of assumptions. The calculation of a company valuation is a lengthy exercise. If you adopt an unconventional approach, it is all too easy to focus on the separate elements of the valuation independently, and inadvertently introduce inconsistencies which render the valuation meaningless; in consequence adopting the generally accepted approach is strongly recommended!

8.3   WHICH CASH FLOWS?

Investors in a company are interested in its value after the prior claims of debt providers have been met. Typically the starting point is the nominal free cash flows after tax available to *all* providers of capital to a company, whether creditors, lenders or shareholders. From this overall valuation of the company, which we call the **enterprise value**, the claims of debt providers are deducted and the market value of any non-core investments is added to give the value that is of interest to investors, the **total equity value** of the company, shown in Table 8.1.

Table 8.1   Determining total equity value
Present value of nominal free cash flows during forecast period
+ Present value of terminal value
= Enterprise value
+ Investments (at market value)
– Debt (at market value)
= Total equity value

This approach is consistent with our separation of operating and financing decisions, as the *cash flow* arising from the company's operations *will not be* affected by its financial structure, although the *value* of the company *will be* affected by the financial structure, since it will be reflected in the company's cost of capital used to arrive at the present value of those cash flows.

The focus on cash flows as against earnings also means that this approach allows you to compare the value of companies in countries which follow different accounting practices.

Investments owned by a company that are not part of the core business are treated separately. These investments should be eliminated from any historical ratios on which the forecasts of the core business will be based, and added separately to the company valuation at their (present) market value.

BOX 8.1   VALUATION OF INVESTMENTS AND NON-CORE ACTIVITIES

The investment in marketable securities held by Blue Circle provides a good example of an investment that is not needed for the company to conduct its core business.

There are no specific grounds for assuming that the company will continue to hold this investment and core operations would not be affected by the disposal of these assets. If these financial assets were included in ratios such as asset turnover or minimum cash/sales that were used as a basis for forecasting the asset investment required to achieve a given level of future sales, that asset investment would be overstated.

Our understanding of the company's core business tells us little about the future performance of the marketable securities. Therefore, rather than looking in detail at the future cash flows arising from the marketable securities you can look at the market's view of their value, which is easily identified in this instance as the current market price of the securities.

The value of the securities can then be added to the present value of the cash flows generated by the company's core activities to give the total value of its core and non-core activities. The total equity value of the company can then be calculated by deducting the market value of debt.

You should note that the historical 'free cash flow' calculated by OUFS deducts depreciation as proxy for maintenance CAPEX. That free cash flow looks at the cash available or 'free' for long-term investments and dividends.

The nominal free cash flow is the difference between all revenues and sources of cash arising from a company's core business following a specific strategy, less all the expenses and investments required to implement the strategy. While detailed definitions may vary slightly from analyst to analyst it will follow a format similar to Table 8.2.

Table 8.2   Free cash flow – valuations
Net operating profit (NOP)
+ Depreciation
= Earnings before interest taxes depreciation and amortisation (EBITDA)
– Taxes
– Expenditure on PP&E (CAPEX)
+/– Change in net operating assets
+/– Change in operating cash
+/– Other
= Free cash flow

An explicit forecast of free cash flow on a nominal basis is prepared for a period that coincides with a full economic cycle and is often about ten years. The present value of the free cash flows can be calculated using the weighted average cost of capital that will reflect the target debt/equity structure. The cash flows arising beyond the horizon of the detailed forecast are estimated as a single residual or terminal value on the basis of techniques to be discussed in Unit 6.

8.4   VALUE DRIVERS

The key financial relationships, or ratios, that determine the elements of free cash flows, as defined above, are often called 'value drivers'.

Arguably, the most important driver of the value of a company is the level of sales revenue that the company can achieve with a given strategy in a specific economic and industrial context.

The first value driver that appears in our calculation is the operating margins, or the level of net operating profit that the enterprise retains. Net operating profit should be adjusted to add back the non-cash deductions. The simple model in Table 8.2 shows only depreciation, but amortisation, depletion and any other non-cash deduction made before the calculation of net operating profit should be treated in the same way.

The appropriate national tax rate may not be as simple as choosing a single published rate, as you will see in Unit 5.

The second value driver is the level of taxes that must be paid on these profits; the rate payable determines the share that remains for the shareholders. It is important to remember that it is cash flow that we are considering and it is the cash taxes *that would be payable if the company had no debt* that should be deducted. Since taxes are often payable in arrears it may be appropriate to assume that the cash taxes actually paid in a given year should relate to the profits earned in the previous year; this is a refinement that you will often see in valuation models. You may be surprised to see taxes payable calculated by applying the national tax rate (rather than the effective tax rate) to net operating profit (rather than profit before tax), but remember that the calculation is based on the assumption that the company that you are valuing has no debt. The saving associated with the 'tax shelter' provided by debt is reflected in the cost of debt included in the discount rate.

The final value drivers included in the free cash flow calculation relate to the investment in operating and fixed assets needed to generate the forecast level of sales. In Table 8.2 we have separated net operating assets from operating cash. Strictly speaking, they are both operating assets; indeed, valuation models often treat them together as 'working capital'. They have been separated because the historical pattern, on which the forecast is usually based, does not allow you to distinguish between cash that was held for operating reasons and cash that was held for investment reasons. A clear pattern of net operating assets excluding cash provides a better base for forecasting net accounts receivable, inventories, trade creditors and accrued and prepaid expenses. The potentially more volatile pattern of investment cash balances is prevented from obscuring the historical patterns.

BOX 8.2   BLUE CIRCLE: FREE CASH FLOW FORECAST

The assumptions that have been set out in the illustrations included in this unit, are very conservative. As investors will enjoy the benefits of a strong performance, it is appropriate that they should take the full range of possible outcomes into account. They typically look at a range of possible forecasts to give a range of possible valuations. The conservative assumptions used in this illustration would be appropriate to estimate the minimum valuation that the investor would expect to realise. Since the mechanics of the calculation do not change, the conservative assumptions set out above will be used for this illustration, but in practice the calculations would be repeated to establish the 'most likely' or 'best case' valuations.

The cash flows for valuing a company are forecast as if the company had no debt. Any reduction in tax payable arising because the company uses debt to finance its activities is reflected in the weighted average cost of capital (WACC) that is used to calculate the present value of the company's future cash flows. The WACC will also reflect the cost of equity finance and the anticipated debt/equity ratio. The forecast cash flows for valuations therefore include tax as if there were no debt and exclude dividend payments. The WACC implies that dividends *must* be paid, in contrast to the debt capacity calculation that *may* assume that dividends are not paid during the forecast period. Since a valuation considers all future cash flows, it must reflect the fact that shareholders will ultimately require a return, as opposed to lenders who may ignore the requirements of shareholders in the short term.

Taxes in this instance should reflect national tax rates applied to operating profit. If the company is operating in several jurisdictions, the weighted average tax rate should be used. This can be a complicated rate to estimate, given the range of possible rates, double taxation agreements, capital allowances and tax prepayments. In practice, it is often necessary to accept a simple assumption and repeat the calculation to ascertain the sensitivity of the valuation to variations in the tax rate. For the purposes of this illustration it is assumed that the UK national tax rate of 30% will apply.

The cash flows should be forecast for a period that reflects a full economic cycle. For the purposes of this illustration the calculations are completed for only five years; this is less than a full economic cycle and the forecast should be made for a further five years if a meaningful valuation is to be calculated. The forecast cash flows needed to calculate the free cash flow to be used as the basis of a company valuation are set out in Table 8.3 (data drawn from Table 7.2). The calculation of the valuation cannot be completed until the WACC, and the terminal value have been calculated; these subjects will be covered in Units 4 and 6 respectively.

Table 8.3   Blue Circle – free cash flow forecast (£m)

	1998	1999	2000	2001	2002
Net operating profit	298.9	312.7	327.3	342.6	358.5
+ Depreciation	104.5	109.5	114.6	120.0	125.7
Subtotal: EBITDA	**403.4**	**422.2**	**442.0**	**462.6**	**484.2**
– Taxes	(89.7)	(93.8)	(98.2)	(102.8)	(107.5)
– Expenditure on P,P&E (capex)	(2.1)	(162.1)	(169.8)	(177.8)	(186.2)
+/–Change in net operating assets	24.2	(15.3)	(16.0)	(16.8)	(17.6)
+/–Change in operating cash	(3.3)	(5.6)	(5.8)	(6.1)	(6.4)
+/–Other	0.0	0.0	0.0	0.0	0.0
Free cash flow	**332.8**	**145.4**	**152.1**	**159.1**	**166.4**

8.5 BROKERS' REPORTS

Perhaps the most widely circulated format of a company valuation is the broker's report. These reports, prepared by analysts working for financial institutions that buy and sell shares for clients, summarise the performance of a company within a sector, evaluate its future prospects, and estimate its value to investors, often using a variety of techniques including discounted cash flow. The valuation on the basis of this analysis is compared with the market price of the shares in order to provide existing and potential shareholders with a buy, sell or hold recommendation at the prevailing market price. A broker's report on Blue Circle reviewing the company's performance in 1996 is included as Appendix 5.

Where brokers' reports are available, they provide a valuable resource for anyone interested in the medium- to long-term prospects of a company. Prepared by analysts with a detailed knowledge of the industrial sector, they can provide a useful 'second opinion' to compare with your own analysis. Brokers' analysts are often able to meet companies, tour their facilities, and discuss a company's operating performance with their peers and trading partners – possibly providing you with information which would not otherwise be available. Remember, however, that there is usually a range of forecasts among the analysts of a sector, and it is not unusual for a company's actual performance to fall outside this range.

Activity 8.1

Read the broker's report on Blue Circle included as Appendix 5.

What new information has the analyst provided?

How does this analysis change your assessment of the company?

Do you feel that this analysis overvalues or undervalues the company, or confirms your assessment? Justify your answer with reference to the specific strengths and weaknesses identified by (or overlooked by) the report.

SUMMARY

This section described an approach to forecasting that might be adopted by the group with the longest time horizon, shareholders.

The process of valuing a company on the basis of future cash flows was reviewed. Discounted cash flow valuations are complex, but are generally accepted to establish the most meaningful estimate of the value of a company to its shareholders.

A discounted cash flow valuation estimates all free cash flows arising from a company's core operations; it discounts these future cash flows to a present value on the basis of a weighted average cost of capital reflecting the target financial structure. This produces a value for the whole enterprise and, after deducting the market value of debt and adding the market value of investment and non-core activities, the value of the company to its shareholders can be established.

SUMMARY AND CONCLUSIONS

In this unit, we outlined the process by which the past performance of a company (as reflected in the Annual Report and the ratios discussed in Unit 2) can be used to form expectations about its future cash flows. We illustrated this by considering three categories of potential users: trading partners, lenders, and investors.

Section 2 discussed the purpose and principles of forecasting. Sections 3 to 5 outlined techniques that analysts can use to calculate future income statements, cash flows and balance sheets. These techniques used both organisations' historical financial ratios and an understanding of the economic environment and industrial context. Sections 6 to 8 looked at the application of forecasting techniques to three categories of users who focus on very different time horizons: trading partners (the short term), lenders (medium term) and shareholders (the long term). We also considered sources of information forecasts prepared by others that may be available to support these three categories of users.

At the end of this unit, you should now be able to:

- describe the basic techniques of forecasting
- prepare simple forecasts
- evaluate and use appropriately forecasts prepared by others.

ANSWERS TO EXERCISES

Exercise 3.1

Boots' pattern of sales growth between 1993 and 1997 has been erratic as the result of the disposals and acquisitions that were made during the period. In these circumstances, it is reasonable to set the historic growth rates to one side and link the growth in the continuing businesses with the rate of growth of the economies in which the company is operating. The chosen reference rates are the rates of growth of nominal GDP in the UK, Europe and total OECD. These reference rates are at best approximations; the EU growth rates include the UK and the distribution of sales in the rest of the world is unlikely to coincide exactly with the weighted growth of all OECD countries. Moreover, as the company has a small share of these overseas markets, the growth in the company's sales could easily exceed the overall rate of growth in those economies. This is in contrast to the position in the UK, where Boots is the dominant retailer of pharmaceuticals and personal care products in a mature market.

Accepting the sales forecast, you must now consider the profit margins, which have historically been quite different in each of the geographical areas. The operating margins have ranged from 10.18% to 12.15% of sales in the UK, while operating margins have fallen from 23.29% in 1993 to 7.35% in 1997 in the rest of the world. Margins have fallen from a high of 3.86% to losses of (4.52%) in the rest of Europe. These margins reflect exceptional gains and losses that should be removed to give a clearer picture of underlying profit margins.

There is no overall trend across the regions, with margins improving in some areas and declining in others. With no trend apparent, you might reasonably assume that margins stay at their current levels in each region. This implies that declining trends in overseas markets will be halted. This assumption might be justified by the observation that it is the company's strategy to invest in these regions through the expansion of their highest margin division, Boots the Chemists.

Group costs (£34.9m in 1997) need to be allocated to one of the regions. The UK, being by far the largest, appears to be the most reasonable choice. In order to get a clearer picture of underlying profit, 1997 exceptional operating income of £8.6m could be deducted from UK operating profit. These two adjustments bring the operating profit in the UK to £490.8m (£534.3m – £34.9m – £8.6m) or 11.16% of 1997 sales in the UK.

Reflecting these assumptions, you might calculate 1998 operating profit as set out in Table A.1.

Table A.1

Region	1998 Sales £m (projected)	1998 Operating Profit /Sales % (projected)	1998 Operating Profit £m (projected)
UK	4598.10	11.16	4598.10 × 0.1116 = 513.15
Rest of Europe	132.38	(4.52)	132.38 × (0.0452) = (5.98)
Rest of world	95.19	7.35	95.19 × 0.0735 = 7.00

Exercise 4.1

Net operating assets as a percentage of sales has gone up and down between 1993 and 1997, with quite a dramatic increase in 1997. The largest factor in the 1997 increase is the build-up of inventories, with inventory days rising from 88.18 days in 1996 to 100.88 days in 1997.

Taking a conservative perspective you might assume that net operating assets to sales percentage will remain at the current level, the highest recorded in that period.

1998 Sales £m (projected – Table A.1)	Net operating Assets/sales % (projected)	Net operating assets £m (projected)
4825.67	10.30	4825.67 × 0.103 = 497.04

Fixed asset turnover (or sales/net property plant, and equipment) has remained fairly stable, ranging from 2.83 in 1993 to 2.58 in 1997. As the group's strategy suggests no significant change in business mix, you might again assume that the fixed asset turnover remains at its most recent level.

1998 Sales £m (projected – Table A.1)	Sales/net property plant and equipment % (projected)	Net property plant and equipment £m (projected)
4825.67	2.58	4825.67/2.58 = 1870.41

Exercise 7.1

In order to forecast the cash flows associated with existing debt it is necessary to make some assumptions. The table below is based on the following assumptions:

(a) Debt repayments are made six months into the financial year, therefore interest is payable on the loan repayment for six months.

(b) Where no detailed information is available, it is assumed that the debt is repayable evenly over the period indicated. In this instance, one third of the debt repayable in the years 3–5 is assumed to be repayable each year (£105.6m/3 = £35.2m per year)

(c) It is assumed that the interest rate payable on loan repayments in 1998 is equal to the forecast LIBOR + 0.375% (typical pricing for short-term debt) as this total includes debt of an original maturity less than one year as well as maturing medium-term debt. Loan repayments in the years 1999–2002, as they are maturing medium-term debt, bear the rate of interest payable on medium term debt (LIBOR + 0.50% or 7.70%). Interest payable on the principal element of debt repayable in years 2–5 is LIBOR + 0.50% (or 7.90% in 1998 and 7.70% thereafter). Interest payable on the principal element of debt repayable beyond 5 years is 10.125% from 1998 to 2002 (representing the interest payable on the bonds due 2017).

(d) For the purpose of calculating the after-tax cost of existing debt, a corporate tax rate of 30% (equal to the 1999 national tax rate and close to the company's effective tax rate) is assumed.

These assumptions are logical, but by no means the only assumptions that you could reasonably make. For example, a more conservative assumption would be that repayments were made at the end of the each period.

Year	1998 £m	1999 £m	2000 £m	2001 £m	2002 £m
Loan repayment	167.9	35.3	35.2	35.2	35.2
Interest on repayment	167.9 × 0.0778/2 = 6.53	35.3 × 0.0770/2 = 1.36	35.2 × 0.0770/2 =1.36	35.2 × 0.0770/2 =1.36	35.2 × 0.0770/2 =1.36
Interest on principal	140.9 × 0.0790 + 95.6 × 0.10125 = 11.15 + 9.68 = 20.81	105.6 × 0.077 + 95.6 × 0.10125 = 8.15 + 9.68 = 17.81	70.4 × 0.077 + 95.6 × 0.10125 = 5.44 + 9.68 = 15.10	35.2 × 0.077 + 95.6 × 0.10125 = 2.73 + 9.68 = 12.39	95.6 × 0.10125 =9.68

After taking into account the tax shelter provided by the interest expense, you would then include the following cash flows in your calculation of cash available to service additional debt:

Year	1998 £m	1999 £m	2000 £m	2001 £m	2002 £m
Current portion of long term debt and leases	167.9	35.3	35.2	35.2	35.2
After tax interest on existing debt	(6.53 + 20.81) (1 − 0.30) = 19.14	(1.36 + 17.81) (1 − 0.30) = 13.42	(1.36 + 15.10) (1 − 0.30) = 11.52	(1.36 + 12.39) (1 − 0.30) = 9.63	(1.36 + 9.68) (1 − 0.30) = 7.73

APPENDIX 1 – OUFS THE BOOTS COMPANY PLC

OPEN UNIVERSITY FINANCIAL SPREADSHEET

Company Name:	The Boots Company PLC				Date: 11-Jun-98
Business:	Retailing,Opticians,ConsumerProds				Analyst: PAS
Currency:	Sterling	Units: Millions ▼			
Domicile:	UK				Auditor: KPMG

	ASSETS	31-Mar-93	31-Mar-94	31-Mar-95	31-Mar-96	31-Mar-97
110	**ASSETS**	**31-Mar-93**	**31-Mar-94**	**31-Mar-95**	**31-Mar-96**	**31-Mar-97**
111	Cash and Deposits	10.9	11.5	14.6	15.3	30.9
112	Marketable Securities	364.1	491.9	1,015.6	893.9	603.0
113	Trade Receivables:					
114	-Net Trade Receivables	187.4	199.2	156.4	181.1	208.8
115	- Recoverable under Contracts					
116	-Other Trade Receivables					
117	*Sub Total Trade Receivables*	187.4	199.2	156.4	181.1	208.8
118	Inventory:					
119	- Raw Materials	32.8	29.4	18.4	18.5	24.8
120	- Work in Progress	23.2	19.1	12.3	10.7	10.3
121	- Finished Goods	479.6	462.1	450.0	487.3	594.2
122	- Advance Payments to Suppliers					
123	- Progress Payments					
124	- Development Properties	17.4	11.0	9.1	5.6	38.0
125	*Sub Total Inventory*	553.0	521.6	489.8	522.1	667.3
127	Tax Receivable:					
128	-ACT Receivable					34.1
129	-Corporation Tax Receivable	63.8	85.0	0.8	5.5	2.2
130	-Other Tax Receivable					
131	*Sub Total Tax Receivable*	63.8	85.0	0.8	5.5	36.3
132	Other Receivables					
133	-Due from Related Companies	0.2	0.2	0.1	0.1	
134	-Other Receivables	35.2	22.3	111.9	110.5	32.5
135	*Sub Total Other Receivables*	35.4	22.5	112.0	110.6	32.5
136	Prepaid Expenses	54.9	55.6	50.3	61.7	69.6
137	Sundry Current Assets					
138	**CURRENT ASSETS**	**1,269.5**	**1,387.3**	**1,839.5**	**1,790.2**	**1,648.4**
139	Net Property, Plant and Equipment:					
140	-Land and Buildings - Freehold	786.1	824.5	846.0	909.3	1,005.4
141	-Long Leasehold					
142	-Short Leasehold					
143	-Plant and Machinery	148.2	147.8	111.5	120.4	167.9
144	-Fixtures and Fittings	422.8	465.4	493.5	513.2	533.8
145	-Other Fixed Assets (Depreciable)					
146	-Other Fixed Assets (Non Depreciable)					
147	-Construction in Progress	40.6	36.2	47.0	81.5	62.6
148	*Sub Total Net Property, Plant and Equipment*	1,397.7	1,473.9	1,498.0	1,624.4	1,769.7
149	Investments:					
150	-Related Company	50.8	37.1	16.6	32.9	
151	-Other					0.5
152	-Loans to Related Companies	20.0	20.0	14.0	13.5	
153	*Sub Total Investments*	70.8	57.1	30.6	46.4	0.5
154	Long Term Trade Receivables:					
155	- Related Companies					
156	-Trade Loans					
157	-Other Trade Receivables					
158	*Sub Total LT Trade Receivables*	0.0	0.0	0.0	0.0	0.0
159	Other Long Term Receivables:					
160	- Related Companies					
161	-Non Trade Loans					
162	-Other LT Receivables	5.4	4.2	4.7	2.2	33.1
163	*Sub Total Other LT Receivables*	5.4	4.2	4.7	2.2	33.1
164	Long TermTax Receivable:					
165	-LT ACT Receivable					100.1
166	-LT Corporation Tax Receivable					
167	-Deferred Tax					
168	-Other LT Tax Receivable					
169	*Sub Total Long Term Tax Receivable*	0.0	0.0	0.0	0.0	100.1
170	Prepaid Expenses					
171	Assets held for Sale (ST & LT)					
172	Sundry Non Current Assets					
173	Intangibles :					
174	Goodwill					
175	-Other Amortising	52.1	51.4	28.7	26.6	33.8
176	-Other Nonamortising					
177	- Other					
178	*Sub Total Intangibles*	52.1	51.4	28.7	26.6	33.8
179	**NON CURRENT ASSETS**	**1,526.0**	**1,586.6**	**1,562.0**	**1,699.6**	**1,937.2**
181	**TOTAL ASSETS**	**2,795.5**	**2,973.9**	**3,401.5**	**3,489.8**	**3,585.6**
183	**NOTES TO THE BALANCE SHEET:**					
184			RESTATED			
185	**Finished Goods-Manufacturing**	60	46.1	24.9	37.5	50.6
186	**Finished Goods - Retailing**	419.6	416	425.1	449.8	543.6
187						
188						

OPEN UNIVERSITY FINANCIAL SPREADSHEET

Company Name:	The Boots Company PLC			Date: 11-Jun-98
Business:	Retailing,Opticians,ConsumerProds			Analyst: PAS
Currency:	Sterling Millions			
Domicile	UK			

		31-Mar-93	31-Mar-94	31-Mar-95	31-Mar-96	31-Mar-97
210	LIABILITIES					
211	Short Term Debt:					
212	- Bank Loans	174.7	131.0	244.2	127.1	114.2
213	- Other	34.0	35.5	44.6	33.3	53.7
214	-Bills of Exchange Payable	5.5	1.7	0.6	0.3	4.5
215	-Current Portion Long Term Debt				114.4	
216	-Current Portion Lease Obligations					
217	Sub Total Short Term Debt	214.2	168.2	289.4	275.1	172.4
218	Trade Creditors	240.3	256.5	264.8	269.6	331.1
219	Accrued Expenses	148.3	168.0	151.5	150.8	144.4
220	Customer Prepayments					
221	Taxes Payable:					
222	-Corporation Tax Payable	120.4	58.2	122.2	128.2	135.8
223	-Other Taxes Payable	45.0	157.9	40.9	42.7	156.0
224	Sub Total Taxes Payable	165.4	216.1	163.1	170.9	291.8
225	Dividends Payable		105.1	110.6	122.0	530.0
226	Due to Related Companies					
227	Other Creditors	129.2	99.1	102.9	103.7	127.5
228	Current Provisions:					
229	-Acquisition					
230	-Restructuring					
231	-Retirement /Employee Benefits					
232	-Other Provisions					
233	Sub Total Current Provisions	0.0	0.0	0.0	0.0	0.0
234	Other Current Liabilities					
235	CURRENT LIABILITIES	897.4	1,013.0	1,082.3	1,092.1	1,597.2
236	Long Term Debt:					
237	-Leases	2.4	3.0	1.2	7.0	15.5
238	-Bank Loans					100.5
239	-Bonds and Debentures	366.7	242.1	218.7	97.3	113.5
240	-Other Long Term Debt	1.0	22.8	4.3	3.9	7.0
241	-Convertible Long Term Debt					
242	-Subordinated Debt					
243	-Redeemable Preference Shares					
244	Sub Total Long Term Debt	370.1	267.9	224.2	108.2	236.5
245	Long Term Taxes Payable:					
246	-Corporation Tax Payable					
247	-Other Taxes Payable					
248	Sub Total Long TermTaxes Payable	0.0	0.0	0.0	0.0	0.0
249	Sundry Non Current Liabilities	14.9	48.0	40.5	42.3	38.4
250	TOTAL LIABILITIES	1,282.4	1,328.9	1,347.0	1,242.6	1,872.1
251	Deferred Taxation	13.7	16.6	14.4	26.1	15.8
252	Long Term Provisions:					
253	-Acquisition					57.3
254	-Restructuring			23.1		
255	-Retirement /Employee Benefits					
256	-Other Provisions	14.2	12.5	10.1	19.6	18.9
257	Sub Total Long Term Provisions	14.2	12.5	33.2	19.6	76.2
258	Minority Interests	6.6	7.3			(0.1)
259	TOTAL LIABILITIES AND PROVISIONS	1,316.9	1,365.3	1,394.6	1,288.3	1,964.0
260	Ordinary Shares	259.5	260.2	237.2	238.4	226.5
261	Preference Shares					
262	Share Premium	196.0	204.6	219.0	226.9	233.7
263	Other Share Related					
264	Consolidation Differences					
265	Foreign Exchange Reserve					
266	Revaluation Reserve	292.2	304.9	310.7	321.4	351.9
267	Other Reserves - Restricted			24.0	24.0	36.8
268	Other Reserves -Unrestricted					
269	Profit and Loss Reserve	730.9	838.9	1,216.0	1,390.8	772.7
270	SHAREHOLDERS' EQUITY	1,478.6	1,608.6	2,006.9	2,201.5	1,621.6
271						
272	TOTAL LIABILITIES & EQUITY	2,795.5	2,973.9	3,401.5	3,489.8	3,585.6
273	Cross Check	0.0	0.0	0.0	0.0	0.0
275	ADDITIONAL BALANCE SHEET INFORMATION:					
276	Contingent Liabilities					
277	Acquisition of Subsidiary net of Cash					
278	Book Value Property, Plant and Equipment Sold (Input Negative)	(27.5)	(29.0)	(21.0)	(33.1)	(41.4)
279	Proceeds from Sale of Property, Plant and Equipment	18.0	27.0	24.5	27.6	36.5
280	Property, Plant and Equipment Revaluation for the year	(223.2)	16.8	6.6	16.0	27.1
281	Foreign Exchange relating to plant	7.9	(0.8)	(3.1)	0.8	(2.4)
282	Number of Shares Issued & Outstanding (In Thousands)	1,038,072.0	1,041,000.0	949,000.0	953,000.0	906,100.0
283	Date of Share Price	31-Mar-93	31-Mar-94	31-Mar-95	31-Mar-96	31-Mar-97
284	Share Price	5.61	6.05	5.82	6.27	7.01
285	Earnings per Share	0.269	0.277	0.657	0.358	0.429
286	Dividends per Share	0.134	0.150	0.170	0.185	0.647
287	No. of Days in Accounting Period	365	365	365	365	365

OPEN UNIVERSITY FINANCIAL SPREADSHEET

Company Name:	The Boots Company PLC		Date: 11-Jun-98
Business:	Retailing,Opticians,ConsumerProds		Analyst: PAS
Currency:	Sterling Millions		
Domicile	UK		

	INCOME STATEMENT	31-Mar-93	31-Mar-94	31-Mar-95	31-Mar-96	31-Mar-97
310	**INCOME STATEMENT**					
311						
312	**TOTAL SALES**	**3,962.1**	**3,754.1**	**3,894.1**	**4,010.4**	**4,565.1**
313	Cost of Goods Sold	(2,120.4)	(2,090.2)	(2,138.8)	(2,161.1)	(2,414.5)
314	Selling & Distribution Expenses	(1,146.7)	(1,057.8)	(1,108.8)	(1,158.7)	(1,376.1)
315	Administrative Expense	(214.7)	(180.3)	(194.3)	(206.7)	(253.1)
316	Other Operating Income	28.8	46.8	88.9	(1.4)	0.1
317	Other Operating Expenses	(87.4)	(57.2)	(18.1)	(27.1)	(21.1)
318	Exceptional Items		73.8	(2.8)	(12.8)	(8.6)
319	*For Information - Included in Operating Profit:*					
320	*Depreciation Manufacturer*	*(102.6)*	*(124.1)*	*(110.2)*	*(102.4)*	*(110.0)*
321	*Trader*					
322	*Amortisation*		*(3.1)*	*(2.8)*	*(2.4)*	*(2.4)*
323	*Operating Leases Property*	*(122.7)*	*(135.4)*	*(145.9)*	*(151.2)*	*(185.9)*
324	*Plant & Equipment*	*(8.6)*	*(8.2)*	*(7.4)*	*(4.4)*	*(5.2)*
325	*Other*					
326	*Personnel*					
327	*Advertising*					
328	*Research & Development*					
329	*Wages & salaries*					
330	*Material Expenses*					
331	*Gain/(Loss) Sale of Fixed Asset*	*(9.5)*	*(2.0)*	*3.5*	*(5.5)*	*(4.9)*
332	*Gain/(Loss) Sale of Associate*					
333	*Gain/(Loss) Sale of Investment*					
334	*Royalty Income*					
335	*Foreign Exchange*					
336	**NET OPERATING PROFIT (NOP)**	**421.7**	**489.2**	**520.2**	**442.6**	**491.8**
337	Interest Expense	(45.3)	(45.0)	(47.0)	(38.9)	(39.3)
338	Interest Provisions (Non Cash)					
339	(Capitalised Interest)	0.1	0.5	1.2	3.2	5.1
340	Interest Income	28.3	29.5	32.7	71.1	49.2
341	Other Financial Income	0.4	11.9	18.5	15.5	29.4
342	Other Financial Expense					
343	Equity Income - Associates					
344	Dividend Income					
345	**PROFIT AFTER FINANCIAL ITEMS**	**405.2**	**486.1**	**525.6**	**493.5**	**536.2**
346	Sundry Income					
347	Sundry Expense					
348	Gain / Loss on Sale of Fixed Assets					
349	Gain / Loss on Sale of Investment					
350	Exceptional Income			298.5	10.5	31.6
351	Exceptional Expense		(54.5)			
352	**PRE TAX PROFIT**	**405.2**	**431.6**	**824.1**	**504.0**	**567.8**
353	Corporation Tax - Domestic	(116.5)	(119.5)	(148.2)	(155.4)	(170.9)
354	Corporation Tax - Overseas	(15.3)	(20.9)	(39.7)	(7.5)	(4.8)
355	Deferred Tax	(1.5)	(3.3)	(4.9)	(11.6)	(4.2)
356	Prior Year Adjustment					
357	Other Tax	8.9	3.4	31.8	11.1	4.9
358	**NET PROFIT AFTER TAX (NPAT)**	**280.8**	**291.3**	**663.1**	**340.6**	**392.8**
359	Extraordinary Income					
360	Extraordinary Expense					
361	Minority Interest - Share of RE	(1.7)	(1.7)	(3.9)		0.5
362	Minority Interest - Dividends Paid					
363	Dividends - Ordinary	(139.0)	(156.0)	(166.4)	(176.4)	(586.1)
364	Dividends - Preference					
365	Dividends - Scrip					
366	**RETAINED PROFIT OR LOSS FOR THE FINANCIAL YEAR**	**140.1**	**133.6**	**492.8**	**164.2**	**(192.8)**
367	*Adjustments to* Prior Year					
368	*Profit & Loss* Goodwill Written Off	(30.4)	(30.4)		(8.6)	(120.1)
369	*Reserve:* Goodwill Written Back	13.4	4.8	413.1	5.3	
370	Foreign Exchange Translation	35.2		(18.5)	3.3	(10.4)
371	Transfer to/from Reserves					(294.8)
372	Other	0.7		(510.3)	10.6	
373	**CHANGE IN PROFIT AND LOSS RESERVE**	**159.0**	**108.0**	**377.1**	**174.8**	**(618.1)**
374	*Other Adjustments* Prior Year					
375	*to Shareholders'* Shares Issued	9.4	0.7	1.0	0.7	0.6
376	*Equity:* Share Issue Premium	115.1	8.6	14.4	7.9	6.8
377	Shares Issued for Scrip Dividends			(24.0)	0.5	0.3
378	Shares Repurchased					(12.8)
379	Preference Shares Issued					
380	Other Share related					
381	Goodwill Written Off					
382	Goodwill Written Back					
383	Foreign Exchange Translation					
384	Revaluation for the Year	(236.1)	12.7	5.8	10.7	30.5
385	Transfer to/from Reserves			24.0		
386	Other					12.8
387	**CHANGE IN SHAREHOLDER'S EQUITY**	**47.4**	**130.0**	**398.3**	**194.6**	**(579.9)**
388	Cross Check Profit & Loss	na	0.0	0.0	0.0	0.0
389	Shareholders Equity	na	0.0	0.0	0.0	0.0

OPEN UNIVERSITY FINANCIAL SPREADSHEET

Company Name:	The Boots Company PLC	Date: 11-Jun-98
Business:	Retailing,Opticians,ConsumerProds	Analyst: PAS
Currency:	Sterling Millions	
Domicile:	UK	

410 RATIO ANALYSIS	Line Reference	31-Mar-93	31-Mar-94	31-Mar-95	31-Mar-96	31-Mar-97
411						
412 **CORE RATIOS**						
413 Return on Sales (NPAT/Sales %)	358/312	7.09	7.76	17.03	8.49	8.60
414 Asset Turnover (Sales/Total Assets)	312/181	1.42	1.26	1.14	1.15	1.27
415 Asset Leverage (Total Assets/Equity)	181/270	1.89	1.85	1.69	1.59	2.21
416 Return on Equity (NPAT/Equity %)	358/270	18.99	18.11	33.04	15.47	24.22
417						
418 **OPERATING EFFICIENCY**						
419 Trade Creditor Days	218*287/313	41.36	44.79	45.19	45.53	50.05
420 Accrued Expenses Days	219*287/313	25.53	29.34	25.85	25.47	21.83
421 Inventory Days	125*287/313	95.19	91.08	83.59	88.18	100.88
422 - Raw Materials Days	119*287/313	5.65	5.13	3.14	3.12	3.75
423 - Work in Progress Days	120*287/313	3.99	3.34	2.10	1.81	1.56
424 - Finished Goods Days	121*287/313	82.56	80.69	76.80	82.30	89.83
425 Trade Receivables Days	117*287/312	17.26	19.37	14.66	16.48	16.69
426 Net Operating Assets (Sterling Millions)	117+125+136-218-219	407	352	280	345	470
427 Net Operating Assets/Sales (%)	426/312	10.26	9.37	7.20	8.59	10.30
428 Net Property Plant & Equipment T/O(Sales/NetPP&E)	312/148	2.83	2.55	2.60	2.47	2.58
429 Cash & Marketable Securities/Sales (%)	111+112/312	9.46	13.41	26.46	22.67	13.89
430 Cash & Marketable Securities/Current Assets (%)	111+112/138	29.54	36.29	56.00	50.79	38.46
431						
432 **FINANCIAL STRUCTURE**						
433 Current Ratio	138/235	1.41	1.37	1.70	1.64	1.03
434 Quick Ratio	138-125/235	0.80	0.85	1.25	1.16	0.61
435 Working Capital (Sterling Millions)	138-235	372	374	757	698	51
436 Gross Gearing (%)	217+244/270	39.52	27.11	25.59	17.41	25.22
437 Net Gearing (%)	217+244-111-112/270	14.16	(4.18)	(25.74)	(23.89)	(13.88)
438 Leverage (Gross)	250/270	0.87	0.83	0.67	0.56	1.15
439 Leverage (Tangible Inc. Contingents)	250+276/270-178	0.90	0.85	0.68	0.57	1.18
440 Leverage (Tangible)	250/270-178	0.90	0.85	0.68	0.57	1.18
441 Total Liabilities / Market Cap	250/486	0.22	0.21	0.24	0.21	0.29
442 Total Debt(ST +LT)/Total Debt + Equity	217+244/217+244+270	0.28	0.21	0.20	0.15	0.20
443 Capital Employed(Sterling Millions)	217+244+248:9+257:8+270	2,099	2,113	2,594	2,647	2,145
444 Total Liabilities/Capital Employed	250/443	0.61	0.63	0.52	0.47	0.87
445 Average Debt (Sterling Millions)	(217+244)/2	na	510.2	474.9	448.5	396.1
446 Int.Expense/Average Debt (%)	337/445	na	8.82	9.90	8.67	9.92
447						
448 **PROFITABILITY**						
449 Sales (Sterling Millions)	312	3,962	3,754	3,894	4,010	4,565
450 Change in Sales (%)	312	na	(5.25)	3.73	2.99	13.83
451 Cost of Goods Sold / Sales (%)	313/312	53.52	55.68	54.92	53.89	52.89
452 Selling & Distribution Expense s / Sales (%)	314/312	28.94	28.18	28.47	28.89	30.14
453 Net Operating Profit / Sales (%)	336/312	10.64	13.03	13.36	11.04	10.77
454 Net Operating Profit/Interest Expense	336/337	9.31	10.87	11.07	11.38	12.51
455 Pre-Tax Profit / Sales (%)	352/312	10.23	11.50	21.16	12.57	12.44
456 Effective Tax Rate (%)	353..357/352	30.70	32.51	19.54	32.42	30.82
457 Net Profit after Tax / Sales (%)	358/312	7.09	7.76	17.03	8.49	8.60
458 Dividends/Net Profit after Tax (%)	362..365/358	49.50	53.55	25.09	51.79	149.21
459						
460 **CASHFLOW RATIOS**						
461 EBITDA / Sales (%)	514/312	na	16.4	16.3	13.6	13.2
462 NOP - Taxes Paid (= NOPAT)(Sterling Millions)	512 - 524	na	381	388	294	297
463 NOPAT/Interest Paid	462/525	na	8.47	8.26	7.56	7.54
464 NOPAT/Interest Paid + CPLTD & L	462/(525+526)	na	8.47	8.26	7.56	1.93
465 NOPAT/Interest Paid + CPLTD & L+ Divs. Paid	462/(525+526+528)	na	3.98	1.87	1.44	0.89
466 Operating Free Cash Flow(OFCF)/Interest Paid	553/525	na	9.31	7.96	5.96	6.94
467 OFCF/Int. Paid + CPLTD &L	553/(525+526)	na	9.31	7.96	5.96	1.77
468 OFCF/Int. Paid + CPLTD &L+Divs. Paid	553/(525+526+528)	na	4.37	1.80	1.14	0.82
469 Net Expenditure Property, Plant & Equipment (Millions)	532	na	(186)	(126)	(214)	230
470 Net Expenditure PP&E/Total Assets (%)	469/181	na	6.25	3.71	6.14	6.43
471 Net Expenditure PP&E/Sales (%)	469/312	na	4.95	3.24	5.34	5.05
472 Depn./Net Expenditure PP&E	(320+321)/469	na	0.67	0.87	0.48	0.48
473 Depreciation/Net PP&E (%)	(320+321)/148	7.34	8.42	7.36	6.30	6.22
474 Years to Repay Debt (Debt/NOPAT-Int. Paid)	(217+244)/(462-525)	na	1.30	1.51	1.50	1.59
475						
476						
477 **MARKET RELATED DATA**						
478 Number of Shares Issued & Outstanding (In Thousands	282	1,038,072	1,041,000	949,000	953,000	906,100
479 Date of Share Price	283	34059	34424	34789	35155	35520
480 Share Price	284	5.61	6.05	5.82	6.27	7.01
481 Earnings per Share	285	0.269	0.277	0.657	0.358	0.429
482 Dividend per Share	286	0.134	0.150	0.170	0.185	0.647
483 Change in Dividend per Share (%)	482	na	11.94	13.33	8.82	249.73
484 Number of Days in Period Days	287	365	365	365	365	365
485 Discretionary Cash Flow per Share	527/478	na	0.48	0.46	0.31	0.26
486 Market Capitalisation (Millions)	478*480	5,824	6,298	5,523	5,975	6,352
487 Price / EBITDA per Share	480/514/478	na	10.2	8.7	10.9	10.5
488 Price / Discretionary Cash Flow per Share	480/527/478	na	12.6	12.5	20.1	27.4
489 Price / Free Cash Flow per Share	480/554/478	na	16.8	16.9	31.0	27.2
490 Price / Book	480/270/478	3.9	3.9	2.8	2.7	3.9

OPEN UNIVERSITY FINANCIAL SPREADSHEET

Company Name:	The Boots Company PLC	Date: 11-Jun-98
Business:	Retailing,Opticians,ConsumerProds	Analyst: PAS
Currency:	Sterling Millions	
Domicile	UK	

	DERIVED CASH FLOW	Line Reference	31-Mar-94	31-Mar-95	31-Mar-96	31-Mar-97
510						
511						
512	NET OPERATING PROFIT (NOP)	336	489.2	520.2	442.6	491.8
513	+ Depreciation / Amortisation	320;321;322	127.2	113.0	104.8	112.4
514	EARNINGS BEFORE INTEREST, TAX, DEP'N & AMORT.(EBITDA)		616.4	633.2	547.4	604.2
515	+/- Δ Trade Receivables	117	(11.8)	42.8	(24.7)	(27.7)
516	+/- Δ Inventory	125	31.4	31.8	(32.3)	(145.2)
517	+/- Δ Trade Creditors	218	16.2	8.3	4.8	61.5
518	+/- Δ Accrued Expenses	219	19.7	(16.5)	(0.7)	(6.4)
519	+/- Δ Prepaid Expenses	136	(0.7)	5.3	(11.4)	(7.9)
520	*Sub Total: Change Net Operating Assets*		54.8	71.7	(64.3)	(125.7)
521	+/- Δ Other Current Assets	137, 135	12.9	(89.5)	1.4	78.1
522	+/- Δ Other Current Liabilities	220,226,227,234	(30.1)	3.8	0.8	23.8
523	OPERATING CASH FLOW (OCF)		654.0	619.2	485.3	580.4
524	- Taxes Paid	224,248,251,353..57,131,169	(107.9)	(132.0)	(148.6)	(195.3)
525	- Interest Paid	337,338	(45.0)	(47.0)	(38.9)	(39.3)
526	- Current Portion Long Term Debt & Leases	215,216	0.0	0.0	0.0	(114.4)
527	DISCRETIONARY CASH FLOW		501.1	440.2	297.8	231.4
528	- Dividends Paid	225,362...365	(50.9)	(160.9)	(165.0)	(178.1)
529	CASH FLOW BEFORE LONG TERM USES (CFBLTU)		450.2	279.3	132.8	53.3
530	- Expenditure on Property, Plant and Equipment	148,320,321,348,339,278,280,281	(212.8)	(150.6)	(241.9)	(266.9)
531	+ Proceeds from Sale of Property, Plant & Equip.	279	27.0	24.5	27.6	36.5
532	*Subtotal Net Expenditure on PP&E*		(185.8)	(126.1)	(214.3)	(230.4)
533	+/- Net Expenditure on Investments	333,343,349,153	13.7	26.5	(15.8)	45.9
534	+ Interest Received	340	29.5	32.7	71.1	49.2
535	+ Dividends Received	344	0.0	0.0	0.0	0.0
536	+/- Δ Intangibles	178,322	(2.4)	19.9	(0.3)	(9.6)
537	+/- Δ Other Long Term Assets	158,163,170,171,172	1.2	(0.5)	2.5	(30.9)
538	+/- Δ Other Long Term Liabilities	249	33.1	(7.5)	1.8	(3.9)
539	+/- Δ Provisions	233,257	(1.7)	20.7	(13.6)	56.6
540	+/- Δ Minority Interests	258,361,362	(1.0)	(11.2)	0.0	0.4
541	+/- Δ Reserves	264..268,280,281,367..372	(28.9)	(89.4)	4.5	(406.7)
542	+ Other Non-core Income	331,333,341,342,346,347	13.9	15.0	21.0	34.3
543	+/- Exceptional / Extraordinary Inome or Expense	350,351,359,360	(54.5)	298.5	10.5	31.6
544	CASH FLOW AFTER INVESTING ACTIVITIES (CFAIA)		267.3	457.9	0.2	(410.2)
545	+/- Δ Share Capital	260..263,365	9.3	(8.6)	9.1	(5.1)
546	+/- Δ Long Term Debt	215,216,244	(102.2)	(43.7)	(1.6)	128.3
547	+/- Δ Short Term Debt	212..214	(46.0)	121.2	(128.7)	11.7
548	CASH FLOW AFTER FINANCING ACTIVITIES (CFAFA)		128.4	526.8	(121.0)	(275.3)
549	CHANGE IN CASH	111,112	(128.4)	(526.8)	121.0	275.3
550			0.0	0.0	0.0	0.0
551	**Adjusted Cash Flow Subtotals:**					
553	Operating Free Cash Flow (OFCF)	523-513+524	418.9	374.2	231.9	272.7
554	Free Cash Flow (FCF)	553+525	373.9	327.2	193.0	233.4
555	Residual Free Cash Flow (RFCF)	554+528	323.0	166.3	28.0	55.3
556	Adjusted Operating Cash Flow (AOCF)	514+520	671.2	704.9	483.1	478.5

OPEN UNIVERSITY FINANCIAL SPREADSHEET

Company Name:	The Boots Company PLC	Date: 11-Jun-98
Business:	Retailing,Opticians,ConsumerProds	Analyst: PAS
Currency:	Sterling Millions	
Domicile:	UK	

	BREAKDOWN BY DIVISION	31-Mar-93	31-Mar-94	31-Mar-95	31-Mar-96	31-Mar-97
610	**BREAKDOWN BY DIVISION**					
611	**SALES BY DIVISION**					
612	Division 1-Boots the Chemist	2,663.9	2,808.0	2,943.4	3,107.6	3,313.5
613	Division 2-Halfords	326.3	356.1	377.1	389.6	411.9
614	Division 3-Boots Healthcare International	124.4	206.8	185.8	190.0	227.4
615	Division 4-Do It All	200.2	194.2	185.3	170.7	301.4
616	Division 5-Other	145.0	274.6	283.0	323.2	357.7
617	Subtotal Continuing Operations	3,459.8	3,839.7	3,974.6	4,181.1	4,611.9
618	Discontinued Operations-Children's World	70.2	84.1	104.8	114.3	12.9
619	Other-Boots Pharmaceuticals	463.2	419.9	426.4		
620	Other-Sephora	69.1	24.5			
621	**TOTAL**	4,062.3	4,368.2	4,505.8	4,295.4	4,624.8
622	**% CHANGE IN SALES**					
623	Division 1-Boots the Chemist		5.41%	4.82%	5.58%	6.63%
624	Division 2-Halfords		9.13%	5.90%	3.31%	5.72%
625	Division 3-Boots Healthcare International		66.24%	(10.15%)	2.26%	19.68%
626	Division 4-Do It All		(3.00%)	(4.58%)	(7.88%)	76.57%
627	Division 5-Other		89.38%	3.06%	14.20%	10.67%
628	Subtotal Continuing Operations		10.98%	3.51%	5.20%	10.30%
629	Discontinued Operations-Children's World		19.80%	24.61%	9.06%	(88.71%)
630	Other-Boots Pharmaceuticals		(9.35%)	1.55%		
631	Other-Sephora		(64.54%)			
632	**TOTAL**		7.53%	3.15%	(4.67%)	7.67%
633	**SALES BY DIVISION AS % OF TOTAL SALES**					
634	Division 1-Boots the Chemist	65.58%	64.28%	65.32%	72.35%	71.65%
635	Division 2-Halfords	8.03%	8.15%	8.37%	9.07%	8.91%
636	Division 3-Boots Healthcare International	3.06%	4.73%	4.12%	4.42%	4.92%
637	Division 4-Do It All	4.93%	4.45%	4.11%	3.97%	6.52%
638	Division 5-Other	3.57%	6.29%	6.28%	7.52%	7.73%
639	Subtotal Continuing Operations	85.17%	87.90%	88.21%	97.34%	99.72%
640	Discontinued Operations-Children's World	1.73%	1.93%	2.33%	2.66%	0.28%
641	Other-Boots Pharmaceuticals	11.40%	9.61%	9.46%		
642	Other-Sephora	1.70%	0.56%			
643	**TOTAL**	100.00%	100.00%	100.00%	100.00%	100.00%
644	**NET OPERATING PROFIT BY DIVISION**					
645	Division 1-Boots the Chemist	285.0	323.9	349.7	384.8	426.5
646	Division 2-Halfords	4.7	14.5	20.5	22.1	26.8
647	Division 3-Boots Healthcare International	2.6	21.3	9.8	(8.2)	(8.9)
648	Division 4-Do It All	(14.4)	(47.2)	(6.3)	(10.1)	(6.9)
649	Division 5-Other	55.0	58.5	62.4	68.2	62.8
650	Subtotal Continuing Operations	332.9	371.0	436.1	456.8	500.3
651	Discontinued Operations-Children's World	(3.3)	(1.6)	0.5	(1.4)	0.1
652	Other-Boots Pharmaceuticals	91.4	44.5	86.4		
653	Other-Sephora	0.2	0.2			
654	**TOTAL**	421.2	414.1	523.0	455.4	500.4
655	**% CHANGE IN NET OPERATING PROFIT BY DIVISION**					
656	Division 1-Boots the Chemist		13.65%	7.97%	10.04%	10.84%
657	Division 2-Halfords		208.51%	41.38%	7.80%	21.27%
658	Division 3-Boots Healthcare International		719.23%	(53.99%)	(183.67%)	(8.54%)
659	Division 4-Do It All		(227.78%)	86.65%	(60.32%)	31.68%
660	Division 5-Other		6.36%	6.67%	9.29%	(7.92%)
661	Subtotal Continuing Operations		11.44%	17.55%	4.75%	9.52%
662	Discontinued Operations-Children's World		51.52%	131.25%	(380.00%)	107.14%
663	Other-Boots Pharmaceuticals		(51.31%)	94.16%		
664	Other-Sephora					
665	**TOTAL**		(1.69%)	26.30%	(12.93%)	9.88%
666	**NET OPERATING PROFIT % OF SALES BY DIVISION**					
667	Division 1-Boots the Chemist	10.70%	11.53%	11.88%	12.38%	12.87%
668	Division 2-Halfords	1.44%	4.07%	5.44%	5.67%	6.51%
669	Division 3-Boots Healthcare International	2.09%	10.30%	5.27%	(4.32%)	(3.91%)
670	Division 4-Do It All	(7.19%)	(24.30%)	(3.40%)	(5.92%)	(2.29%)
671	Division 5 Other	37.93%	21.30%	22.05%	21.10%	17.56%
672	Subtotal Continuing Operations	9.62%	9.66%	10.97%	10.93%	10.85%
673	Discontinued Operations-Children's World	(4.70%)	(1.90%)	0.48%	(1.22%)	0.78%
674	Other-Boots Pharmaceuticals	19.73%	10.60%	20.26%		
675	Other-Sephora	0.29%	0.82%			
676	**TOTAL**	10.37%	9.48%	11.61%	10.60%	10.82%

OPEN UNIVERSITY FINANCIAL SPREADSHEET

Company Name:	The Boots Company PLC	Date: 11-Jun-98
Business:	Retailing,Opticians,ConsumerProds	Analyst: PAS
Currency:	Sterling Millions	
Domicile:	UK	

	BREAKDOWN BY AREA	31-Mar-93	31-Mar-94	31-Mar-95	31-Mar-96	31-Mar-97
710						
711	**SALES BY AREA**					
712	Area 1-UK	3,396.1	3,783.4	3,937.9	4,016.0	4,395.9
713	Area 2-Rest of Europe	243.	81.	61.8	81.3	126.2
714	Area 3-Rest ofWorld	322.4	83.3	79.7	83.8	89.8
715	Area 4-Group Costs					
716	Area 5					
717	Subtotal Continuing Operations	3,962.1	3,948.3	4,079.4	4,181.1	4,611.9
718	Discontinued Operations-UK		26.1	22.9	114.3	12.9
719	Discontinued Operations-Rest of Europe		126.9	131.1		
720	Discontinued Operations-Rest of World		266.9	272.4		
721	**TOTAL**	3,962.1	4,368.2	4,505.8	4,295.4	4,624.8
722	**% CHANGE IN SALES**					
723	Area 1-UK		11.40%	4.08%	1.98%	9.46%
724	Area 2-Rest of Europe		(66.50%)	(24.26%)	31.55%	55.23%
725	Area 3-Rest ofWorld		(74.16%)	(4.32%)	5.14%	7.16%
726	Area 4-Group Costs					
727	Area 5					
728	Subtotal Continuing Operations		(0.35%)	3.32%	2.49%	10.30%
729	Discontinued Operations-UK			(12.26%)	399.13%	(88.71%)
730	Discontinued Operations-Rest of Europe			3.31%		
731	Discontinued Operations-Rest of World			2.06%		
732	**TOTAL**		10.25%	3.15%	(4.67%)	7.67%
733	**SALES BY AREA AS % OF TOTAL SALES**					
734	Area 1-UK	85.71%	86.61%	87.40%	93.50%	95.05%
735	Area 2-Rest of Europe	6.15%	1.87%	1.37%	1.89%	2.73%
736	Area 3-Rest ofWorld	8.14%	1.91%	1.77%	1.95%	1.94%
737	Area 4-Group Costs					
738	Area 5					
739	Subtotal Continuing Operations	100.00%	90.39%	90.54%	97.34%	99.72%
740	Discontinued Operations-UK		0.60%	0.51%	2.66%	0.28%
741	Discontinued Operations-Rest of Europe		2.91%	2.91%		
742	Discontinued Operations-Rest of World		6.11%	6.05%		
743	**TOTAL**	100.00%	100.00%	100.00%	100.00%	100.00%
744	**NET OPERATING PROFIT BY AREA**					
745	Area 1-UK	358.5	385.1	449.0	477.1	534.3
746	Area 2-Rest of Europe	9.4	2.7	1.8	(1.0)	(5.7)
747	Area 3-Rest ofWorld	75.1	12.1	10.	7.8	6.
748	Area 4-Group Costs	(21.8)	(30.3)	(24.8)	(27.1)	(34.9)
749	Area 5					
750	Subtotal Continuing Operations	421.2	369.	436.	456.8	500.3
751	Discontinued Operations-UK		(43.7)	(27.4)	(1.4)	0.1
752	Discontinued Operations-Rest of Europe		9.2	16.7		
753	Discontinued Operations-Rest of World		79.0	97.1		
754	**TOTAL**	421.2	414.1	523.0	455.4	500.4
755	**% CHANGE IN NET OPERATING PROFIT BY AREA**					
756	Area 1-UK		7.42%	16.59%	6.26%	11.99%
757	Area 2-Rest of Europe		(71.28%)	(33.33%)	(155.56%)	(470.00%)
758	Area 3-Rest ofWorld		(83.89%)	(12.40%)	(26.42%)	(15.38%)
759	Area 4-Group Costs		(38.99%)	18.15%	(9.27%)	(28.78%)
760	Area 5					
761	Subtotal Continuing Operations		(12.25%)	18.13%	4.63%	9.52%
762	Discontinued Operations-UK			37.30%	94.89%	107.14%
763	Discontinued Operations-Rest of Europe			81.52%		
764	Discontinued Operations-Rest of World			22.91%		
765	**TOTAL**		(1.69%)	26.30%	(12.93%)	9.88%
766	**NET OPERATING PROFIT % OF SALES BY AREA**					
767	Area 1-UK	10.56%	10.18%	11.40%	11.88%	12.15%
768	Area 2-Rest of Europe	3.86%	3.31%	2.91%	(1.23%)	(4.52%)
769	Area 3-Rest ofWorld	23.29%	14.53%	13.30%	9.31%	7.35%
770	Area 4-Group Costs					
771	Area 5					
772	Subtotal Continuing Operations	10.63%	9.36%	10.70%	10.93%	10.85%
773	Discontinued Operations-UK		(167.43%)	(119.65%)	(1.22%)	0.78%
774	Discontinued Operations-Rest of Europe		7.25%	12.74%		
775	Discontinued Operations-Rest of World		29.60%	35.65%		
776	**TOTAL**	10.63%	9.48%	11.61%	10.60%	10.82%

OPEN UNIVERSITY FINANCIAL SPREADSHEET

Company Name:	The Boots Company PLC	Date: 11-Jun-98
Business:	Retailing,Opticians,ConsumerProds	Analyst: PAS
Currency:	Sterling Millions	
Domicile:	UK	

	SUMMARY		31-Mar-93	31-Mar-94	31-Mar-95	31-Mar-96	31-Mar-97
809							
810							
811	A S S E T S	Line Reference					
812	Cash. Deposits and Marketable Securities	111+112	375.0	503.4	1,030.2	909.2	633.9
813	Trade Receivables	117	187.4	199.2	156.4	181.1	208.8
814	Inventory	125	553.0	521.6	489.8	522.1	667.3
815	Other Current Assets	131+135+136+137	154.1	163.1	163.1	177.8	138.4
816	Current Assets	130	1,269.5	1,387.3	1,839.5	1,790.2	1,648.4
817	Net Property, Plant and Equipment	148	1,397.7	1,473.9	1,498.0	1,624.4	1,769.7
818	Investments	153	70.8	57.1	30.6	46.4	0.5
819	Long Term Receivables	158+163	5.4	4.2	4.7	2.2	33.1
820	Other Long Term Assets	169+170:172	0.0	0.0	0.0	0.0	100.1
821	Intangibles	178	52.1	51.4	28.7	26.6	33.8
822	Non Current Assets	179	1,526.0	1,586.6	1,562.0	1,699.6	1,937.2
823	TOTAL ASSETS	181	2,795.5	2,973.9	3,401.5	3,489.8	3,585.6
824							
825	LIABILITIES						
826	Short Term Debt	217	214.2	168.2	289.4	275.1	172.4
827	Trade Creditors	218	240.3	256.5	264.8	269.6	331.1
828	Accrued Expenses	219	148.3	168.0	151.5	150.8	144.4
829	Other Current Liabilities	220+224:7+233+234	294.6	420.3	376.6	396.6	949.3
830	Current Liabilities	235	897.4	1,013.0	1,082.3	1,092.1	1,597.2
831	Long Term Debt	244	370.1	267.9	224.2	108.2	236.5
832	Other Non Current Liabilities	248+249	14.9	48.0	40.5	42.3	38.4
833	Total Liabilities	250	1,282.4	1,328.9	1,347.0	1,242.6	1,872.1
834	Deferred Taxatio	251	13.7	16.6	14.4	26.1	15.8
835	Long Term Provisions:	257	14.2	12.5	33.2	19.6	76.2
836	Minority Interests	258	6.6	7.3	0.0	0.0	(0.1)
837	Total Liabilities and Provisions	259	1,316.9	1,365.3	1,394.6	1,288.3	1,964.0
838	Share Capital	260:263	455.5	464.8	456.2	465.3	460.2
839	Other Reserves	264:268	292.2	304.9	334.7	345.4	388.7
840	Profit and Loss Reserve	269	730.9	838.9	1,216.0	1,390.8	772.7
841	Shareholder's Equity	270	1,478.6	1,608.6	2,006.9	2,201.5	1,621.6
842	TOTAL LIABILITIES & EQUITY	272	2,795.5	2,973.9	3,401.5	3,489.8	3,585.6
843							
844	INCOME STATEMENT						
845	TOTAL SALES	312	3,962.1	3,754.1	3,894.1	4,010.4	4,565.1
846	Cost of Goods Sold	313	(2,120.4)	(2,090.2)	(2,138.8)	(2,161.1)	(2,414.5)
847	Selling & Distribution Expenses	314	(1,146.7)	(1,057.8)	(1,108.8)	(1,158.7)	(1,376.1)
848	Administrative Expense	315	(214.7)	(180.3)	(194.3)	(206.7)	(253.1)
849	Other Operating Income/Expenses	316:317	(58.6)	(10.4)	70.8	(28.5)	(21.0)
850	Exceptional Items	318	0.0	73.8	(2.8)	(12.8)	(8.6)
851	NET OPERATING PROFIT (NOP)	336	421.7	489.2	520.2	442.6	491.8
852	Net Interest Expense	337:340	(16.9)	(15.0)	(13.1)	35.4	15.0
853	Other Financial Income/Expense	341:344	0.4	11.9	18.5	15.5	29.4
854	PROFIT AFTER FINANCIAL ITEMS	345	405.2	486.1	525.6	493.5	536.2
855	Other Income/Expense	346:349	0.0	0.0	0.0	0.0	0.0
856	Exceptional Income/Expense	350+351	0.0	(54.5)	298.5	10.5	31.6
857	PRE TAX PROFIT	352	405.2	431.6	824.1	504.0	567.8
858	Taxes	353:357	(124.4)	(140.3)	(161.0)	(163.4)	(175.0)
859	NET PROFIT AFTER TAX (NPAT)	358	280.8	291.3	663.1	340.6	392.8
860	Extraordinary Income/Expense	359+360	0.0	0.0	0.0	0.0	0.0
861	Minority Interest	361	(1.7)	(1.7)	(3.9)	0.0	0.5
862	Dividends	362:365	(139.0)	(156.0)	(166.4)	(176.4)	(586.1)
863	RETAINED PROFIT OR LOSS FOR THE YEAR	366	140.1	133.6	492.8	164.2	(192.8)
864							
865	RATIO SUMMARY						
866	Return on Equity (NPAT/Equity %)	416	18.99	18.11	33.04	15.47	24.22
867	Return on Sales (NPAT/Sales %)	413	7.09	7.76	17.03	8.49	8.60
868	Asset Turnover (Sales/Total Assets)	414	1.42	1.26	1.14	1.15	1.27
869	Asset Leverage (Total Assets/Equity)	415	1.89	1.85	1.69	1.59	2.21
870	Net Operating Assets/Sales (%)	427	10.26	9.37	7.20	8.59	10.30
871	Current Ratio	433	1.41	1.37	1.70	1.64	1.03
872	Gross Gearing (%)	436	39.52	27.11	25.59	17.41	25.22
873	Leverage (Gross)	438	0.87	0.83	0.67	0.56	1.15
874	Net Operating Profit / Sales (%)	453	10.64	13.03	13.36	11.04	10.77
875	Net Operating Profit/Interest Expense	454	9.3	10.9	11.1	11.4	12.5
876	NOP - Taxes Paid (= NOPAT)(Sterling Millions)	462	a	381.3	388.2	294.0	296.5
877	NOPAT/Interest Paid + CPLTD & L+ Divs. Paid	465	a	3.98	1.87	1.44	0.89
878	Operating Free Cash Flow (OFCF)	553	a	418.9	374.2	231.9	272.7
879	OFCF/Int. Paid + CPLTD &L+Divs. Paid	468	a	4.37	1.80	1.14	0.82
880	Market Capitalisation (Millions)	486	5,823.6	6,298.1	5,523.2	5,975.3	6,351.8

APPENDIX 2 – EXTRACT FROM THE ANNUAL REPORT 1997, THE BOOTS COMPANY PLC

Chairman's Statement

Boots goes from strength to strength. In a very active year we made good progress on a wide number of fronts, continued to broaden the scope of the business, and significantly increased sales, profits and earnings per share. More importantly total shareholder return over the last five years has averaged 11.8 per cent compound return per annum.

Dividend The board has proposed a final dividend of 14.3p. This is in addition to the declared special interim dividend of 44.2p and brings the total dividend for the year to 64.7p per share. The special dividend has had no influence on the size of the proposed final dividend. The first interim and proposed final together amount to 20.5p per share, an increase of 10.8 per cent over last year. The pro forma ratio of debt to equity based on the 31st March 1997 group balance sheet is 10.5 per cent.

Strategy We maintain a high level of investment in growing and extending our core businesses, and in increasing their efficiency and competitiveness. Boots The Chemists (BTC) is still demonstrating that there is room for growth in the UK through judicious choice of store formats, and has begun a carefully planned international expansion. Halfords and A G Stanley are both shifting their emphasis from high streets to larger, out of town sites, and Boots Opticians continues to expand. All these businesses are benefiting from continued development of own brand and exclusive ranges. Boots Healthcare International (BHI) and Boots Contract Manufacturing (BCM) are extending their presence overseas, both organically and by acquisition.

Healthcare is at the heart of several of our businesses, so the new Labour government and

its plans for the NHS have a significant bearing on the company. We believe the role pharmacies play in the community is one of the pillars of the NHS, and we strongly support policies which will enhance that role.

Acquisitions and disposals In May 1996 we completed the sale of Childrens World to Storehouse for £62.5 million. We judged that we could realise greater value for shareholders by selling the business rather than continuing to invest in it, and, after provision for disposal and other termination costs, the sale adds an exceptional profit of £15 million to this year's accounts.

In June we announced the acquisition of W H Smith's 50 per cent share of Do It All. This included a £50 million contribution from W H Smith which has helped to accelerate the disposal of the 65 stores that Do It All did not wish to keep. We are already having considerable success in turning the business around.

During the year we made two European acquisitions to give BHI a strong platform for international expansion in skincare: Laboratoires Lutsia in France for £115 million, and Farmila Dermical in Italy for £4.1 million.

BCM has also increased its presence in Europe, buying Roval, one of France's leading suppliers of own brand toiletries, for £15.2 million in March 1997.

In the same month we announced an agreement with BASF that largely completes the transfer of products resulting from BASF's purchase of Boots Pharmaceuticals in 1995. This gives us control of key healthcare products in India, Pakistan and Canada and allows us to close manufacturing operations in Australia and South Africa.

2 The Boots Company PLC

The Millennium We fully recognise the importance of putting in place the business systems for this event. We estimate that some 300 man years of effort are required to amend or update our systems across the group. We believe this may be less than for some comparable organisations since we have a progressive plan of systems enhancement and replacement and therefore have been working on the programme for some considerable time.

Preparation for the Millennium is not, however, simply an information technology issue. We have designated managers in each of our businesses to handle this, in close co-operation with our suppliers of products and services. Obviously we seek to ensure that our normal business operations are not disrupted as systems changes are made.

European Monetary Union This is a serious issue for retailers, who will be at the front line in managing the transition for consumers if and when it comes. We are acutely conscious of the potential impact and we have a team examining the implications for our business. The scale of cost for all retailers would be considerably greater than that relating to the Millennium.

People This year we have made the first in a series of planned changes to the board, which will maintain effective control as the business develops. David Thompson, group finance director, and Steve Russell, managing director of BTC, have been appointed to the newly created posts of joint group managing director. Both retain their existing responsibilities and Steve Russell takes on additional responsibility for international retail development. Subject to my reappointment as a director at the annual general meeting, I will extend my term of office for a further year until July 1998. Lord Blyth will then become executive chairman and I will become deputy chairman.

Brian Whalan, a group executive director and managing director of Halfords, will be taking early retirement for personal reasons after the annual general meeting. Brian has made a significant contribution to the company's fortunes, leading many initiatives and running several important businesses. We are grateful for all he has done and wish him a long and happy retirement.

Our ability to go on creating value, year on year, depends on our people: on their understanding of value creation and their commitment to it, on their ideas and initiatives, and on the energy they devote to Boots success. The board and I thank them for their achievements.

In March this year we were honoured to welcome Her Majesty The Queen to our main Nottingham site, where she officially opened BHI's refurbished head office and laid the foundation stone for BTC's head office extension. The BTC building, now over 30 years old, is still an exemplary open plan working environment. In 1996 it became the fourth listed building on the site – further recognition of Boots long-standing commitment to good architecture and design, and improving working conditions for our people.

Michael Angus

Sir Michael Angus
Chairman

3 The Boots Company PLC

Chief Executive's Review

Group sales from continuing businesses increased by 13.8 per cent to £4,565.1 million, and profit before tax and exceptional items was £536.2 million. This was another very good year, in a UK retail market where consumer confidence was slowly reviving but competition remained tough.

Own brand products are playing an increasingly important part in virtually all our operations – not only improving margins but also giving us greater differentiation and a competitive edge in the marketplace. Boots The Chemists (BTC) has a particular advantage through its vertical integration with Boots Contract Manufacturing (BCM), which enables it to exploit market opportunities adroitly. Halfords growing range of own brand products is significantly increasing profitability, and Boots Opticians innovative own brand ranges provide real strength in a very competitive market.

Our sales growth has been aided by continued investment in new stores. BTC opened 26 new small stores, four large stores and five edge of town stores. We also opened 28 edge of town Halfords stores and 13 new Boots Opticians.

Cash flow Operating cash flow amounted to £515.1 million, a decline of £21.4 million from last year. Boots Healthcare International (BHI) and BCM expanded overseas with acquisitions totalling £134.3 million. The disposal of Childrens World together with a final sum from the sale of Boots Pharmaceuticals contributed £135.5 million. Investment in capital expenditure totalled £222.8 million in line with last year. In June 1996, the company's second share repurchase was undertaken, returning £300 million to shareholders. Net funds at 31st March 1997 were £229.5 million.

Businesses BTC continued to make very good progress, increasing sales by 6.6 per cent and operating profit by 10.8 per cent to £426.5 million. Its greater focus on the core health and beauty areas is delivering some outstanding results – particularly in cosmetics, where sales grew almost 20 per cent. The Boots Advantage Card has had highly successful trials in Norwich and Plymouth and we have decided to introduce it nationally. There will be a substantial short term revenue cost, but we will gain an excellent customer database which will give us a lasting competitive advantage.

Halfords significantly improved margins, largely through an increased proportion of own brand sales, and managed a 21.3 per cent increase in operating profit to £26.8 million on a sales increase of 5.7 per cent. The garage servicing business again reduced its losses and is moving towards breakeven trading.

Boots Opticians again performed well, increasing sales by 11.9 per cent and operating profit before exceptionals by 26.6 per cent to £13.8 million. This continued progress is due in large measure to flair and innovation in the development of its own brand ranges.

Our DIY and home decorating businesses, while both still suffering from market overcapacity, are steadily improving. Do It All cut its losses by virtually two-thirds to £6.9 million, with sales up 6.6 per cent on a like for like basis, and succeeded in disposing of 27 underperforming stores during the year. A G Stanley's losses reduced only marginally to £11.8 million, but a substantial proportion of this amount was accounted for by rationalisation costs. It closed a further 35 unprofitable stores in its continuing shift from high streets to large out of town units – where sales increased over 12 per cent during the year.

4 The Boots Company PLC

BCM increased sales by 8.4 per cent and profits before exceptional charges by 26.9 per cent to £21.2 million. While it remains a vital strategic asset to both BTC and BHI, it now also has a substantial third-party business in Europe.

We continue to invest heavily in BHI, a rapidly expanding business. Although sales grew 21.0 per cent, at comparable exchange rates, to £243.4 million during the year, the cost of investment in further growth resulted in a small loss of £6.6 million before exceptionals. This result masks another excellent performance, and we intend to continue reinvesting in this business to maintain its expansion into new territories and line extensions. BHI's acquisition of two European skincare companies will enable it to grow its international over the counter business in pharmacy skincare.

Boots Properties increased its trading profit to £72.1 million on virtually unchanged sales. The business has begun selling some properties – raising an exceptional profit of £14.4 million – as the current stage of the market cycle makes it advantageous to sell rather than hold. Its strategy is to take appropriate advantage of each stage in the market cycle, exploiting the excellent market intelligence it gains from its role as landlord to our retailing businesses.

Extending the Boots franchise We intend to pursue international retailing opportunities more aggressively over the next few years. BTC opened two successful stores in the Republic of Ireland during the year and intends to develop a chain there. This year we will open test BTC stores in The Netherlands and Thailand. In the UK, BTC is exploring opportunities to add value and differentiate itself further from the competition.

Outlook The themes of this report – investment, growth and expansion – indicate the confidence with which the company is moving forward. We are actively seeking new opportunities and setting 'stretch' targets for our businesses, challenging them to innovate and test their capabilities to the utmost. As a business, Boots is still far from mature: indeed, we are constantly delighted to find how much more we can do.

Lord Blyth of Rowington
Deputy Chairman and Chief Executive

5 The Boots Company PLC

Financial Review

Shareholder returns of The Boots Company compared with peer companies
Returns are calculated using average
share prices over the three months to 31st March

Five years to 31st March 1997		%
1	SmithKline Beecham	112.2
2	GUS	109.8
3	Marks & Spencer	80.1
4	Boots	74.6
5	Tesco	63.1
6	Kingfisher	53.9
7	Smith & Nephew	46.7
8	Reckitt & Colman	30.0
9	W H Smith	19.4
10	Sears	9.6
11	J Sainsbury	8.9

Performance measurement We believe that the best overall measure of group performance is total return to shareholders which equates to gross dividends paid plus the movement in the share price. We monitor our performance on a rolling five year basis against ten peer companies, the results of which are shown in the table above.

During the year our share price rose from 599p at the start of the year to 675p on 31st March 1997, giving a market capitalisation of £6.1 billion. The share price ranged from a high of 701p to a low of 555p.

Sales and operating profits from continuing operations before exceptional items increased in the year by 13.8 per cent and 10.7 per cent respectively.

Basic earnings per share (EPS) increased from 35.8p to 42.9p. After adjusting for exceptional items EPS rose from 34.7p to 39.5p. The board has proposed a final dividend of 14.3p. This is in addition to the declared special second interim dividend of 44.2p and brings the total dividend for the year to 64.7p per share. The special dividend has had no influence on the size of the proposed final dividend. The first interim and proposed final together amount to 20.5p per share, an increase of 10.8 per cent over last year.

Cash flow Cash management is one of the key performance measures used by the company to monitor its businesses. The maximisation of cash flow is the key factor in value creation. Free cash flow is defined as the cash flow available to all the providers of capital. The summary of cash flows shown below demonstrates the company's ability consistently to generate a healthy free cash flow.

Summary of cash flows	1997 £m	1996 £m
Operating cash flow before exceptional cash flows	539.9	523.7
Exceptional operating cash flows	(24.8)	12.8
Acquisition of businesses	(170.3)	(41.7)
Disposal of businesses	129.9	(6.7)
Purchase of fixed assets	(222.8)	(225.1)
Disposal of fixed assets	53.9	27.8
Taxation paid	(174.4)	(152.7)
Other items	7.1	9.1
Free cash flow	**138.5**	147.2
Share repurchase	(300.0)	–
Dividends paid	(169.8)	(154.4)
Net interest	39.1	16.2
Net cash flow (page 53)	**(292.2)**	9.0

The group generated cash from operating activities of £539.9 million, an increase of £16.2 million on last year. This figure was adversely affected by £39.8 million due to a change in the law requiring the group to bring forward the payment of VAT.

The exceptional cash flows are analysed in note 22 to the financial statements and include

6 The Boots Company PLC

Free cash flow £m	92/93	290.4
Includes the sale of Boots Pharmaceuticals	93/94	337.4
in 1994/95	94/95	1,161.9
	95/96	147.2
	96/97	138.5

Payment to shareholders £m	92/93	215.1
1992/93 includes a second interim dividend	93/94	47.6
rather than payment of a final dividend in 1993/94.	94/95	663.4
£511.3 million share repurchase in 1994/95,	95/96	154.4
£300 million in 1996/97	96/97	469.8

expenditure on terminating onerous contracts at Do It All of £35.1 million. These relate mainly to property lease commitments.

Investment in fixed assets was at a similar level to last year. The fixed asset disposal proceeds relate mainly to the sale of non-core properties.

The above graph on free cash flow shows the amounts generated by the group for each of the last five years.

Acquisitions and disposals of businesses Boots Healthcare International increased its presence in the European skincare market with the acquisition of Laboratoires Lutsia in France and Farmila Dermical in Italy for a total of £119.1 million.

Boots Contract Manufacturing also expanded in Europe with the acquisition of Roval, the leading supplier of own brand toiletries in France, for £15.2 million.

The proceeds received in the year related to the sale of Childrens World in May 1996 and the final receipt from the sale of Boots Pharmaceuticals which took place in March 1995.

Interest Net interest receivable for 1996/97 was £44.4 million compared with £50.9 million last year. The main reasons for the decrease are the effects of the share repurchase and the acquisition of businesses offset by proceeds on disposal of businesses.

Given the cash, borrowing and interest rate swap position of the group, each one per cent average increase or decrease in short term interest rates increases or decreases net interest payable by about £8 million.

Liquidity and funding At 31st March 1997 net funds were £229.5 million compared with £526.2 million at the start of the year.

7 The Boots Company PLC

The US$175 million bond, raised in 1990, was repaid during the year. It was replaced by a £150 million fixed rate amortising financing, £95 million of which was swapped into a floating rate of interest.

Other short term financing needs are met by commercial paper and short term bank borrowings.

The profile of the group's borrowings gives maturities of two to five years for 45 per cent and more than five years for 40 per cent.

Capital structure The group has undertaken a number of transactions to help achieve a more efficient capital structure, in line with the policy of delivering shareholder value. It is sensible for companies to finance a proportion of their capital requirements with borrowings, and this is especially so when the business consistently produces strong cash flows.

A £300 million share repurchase was implemented in June 1996, bringing the aggregate amount for these transactions over the last three years to some £811 million. They have proved to be a good investment for remaining shareholders, as the share price and dividends have risen subsequently.

Payments to shareholders in the form of dividends and share repurchases over the last five years are shown above.

Following the tax changes introduced last year relating to share repurchases, the board believes that a special dividend is now a better way of creating a more efficient capital structure and delivering more value. All shareholders on the register on 4th June 1997 will receive the tax credits of 11.05p per share which accompany this dividend. These tax credits, for which clearance has been received from the Inland Revenue, will amount to £100.1 million.

Financial Review

In deciding the amount of the special dividend, the board has taken account of the strength of the company's balance sheet, projected future cash flows and capital investment plans. The pro forma ratio of debt to equity based on the 31st March 1997 group balance sheet is 10.5%.

The special dividend payment has had no influence on the size or timing of the final dividend for the year to 31st March 1997, which is being recommended by the directors and considered at the annual general meeting in July, nor will it influence the size of future dividends.

The special dividend, together with the proposed final dividend, other normal dividend payments and the two past share repurchases, will bring the total amount of cash returned to shareholders over the past three years to more than £1.7 billion.

Treasury control policy We have clear principles covering all major aspects of treasury policy. These aim to benefit long term shareholders. Strict guidelines for cash investments apply worldwide, and investments are made only in high quality bank deposits and other liquid instruments.

Controls are in place which seek to prevent fraud and other unauthorised transactions and minimise counterparty risk. There are regular reviews by the group's internal audit staff.

Interest rate policy We continue to believe that hedging the impact of short term movements in interest rates does not increase the worth of the company and that long term shareholders do not ascribe value to the reduction in earnings volatility resulting from such hedging.

In common with other UK retailers, the group has significant liabilities through its obligations to pay rents under property leases, the implicit interest

8 The Boots Company PLC

rate on which can be considered to be fixed.

Some years ago the board adopted a strategy of regular long term interest rate swaps in order to change the balance between fixed and floating rate debt. This activity is strictly controlled and monitored, each swap being authorised by the group finance director.

At the year end the total volume of interest rate swaps on leases was £675 million, with £325 million being undertaken during this year. All of these swaps were done with a maturity of ten years to match the long term nature of the underlying property leases. Further details are given in note 18 on page 68.

Currency exposure policy Modest sales and purchases are made in a range of currencies, but it is not considered that hedging them into sterling adds value.

Taxation The effective tax rate for the group was 31.2 per cent. The main reason for the reduction from the UK standard rate of 33 per cent is the level of capital gains in the year which can either be set against capital losses or rolled over for future capital expenditure.

Pensions The next actuarial valuation of the principal UK pension scheme will be completed as at 1st April 1998. Following the previous valuation there is no requirement for the company to contribute to the scheme although a charge of £4 million has been taken in the year.

Accounting Standards The company fully supports the objectives of the Accounting Standards Board (ASB) in its aim to improve the quality and consistency of financial statements. Over the past twelve months we have commented on ASB pronouncements relevant to our business and we will continue to do so in the future. We are concerned where International Standards depart significantly from UK practice and support the ASB in trying to influence proposed changes on major issues affecting UK practice.

Going concern After making enquiries the directors have a reasonable expectation that the group has adequate resources to continue in operational existence for the foreseeable future. For this reason they continue to adopt the going concern basis in preparing these financial statements.

David Thompson
Joint Group Managing Director
and Finance Director

9 The Boots Company PLC

The Company Today

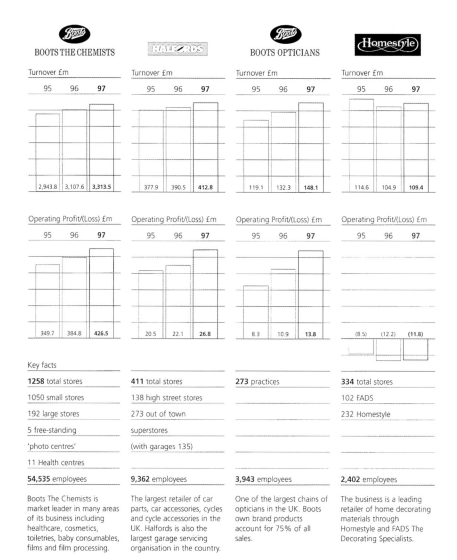

BOOTS THE CHEMISTS

Turnover £m

95	96	**97**
2,943.8	3,107.6	**3,313.5**

Operating Profit/(Loss) £m

95	96	**97**
349.7	384.8	**426.5**

Key facts

1258 total stores

1050 small stores

192 large stores

5 free-standing

'photo centres'

11 Health centres

54,535 employees

Boots The Chemists is market leader in many areas of its business including healthcare, cosmetics, toiletries, baby consumables, films and film processing.

HALFORDS

Turnover £m

95	96	**97**
377.9	390.5	**412.8**

Operating Profit/(Loss) £m

95	96	**97**
20.5	22.1	**26.8**

411 total stores

138 high street stores

273 out of town

superstores

(with garages 135)

9,362 employees

The largest retailer of car parts, car accessories, cycles and cycle accessories in the UK. Halfords is also the largest garage servicing organisation in the country.

BOOTS OPTICIANS

Turnover £m

95	96	**97**
119.1	132.3	**148.1**

Operating Profit/(Loss) £m

95	96	**97**
8.3	10.9	**13.8**

273 practices

3,943 employees

One of the largest chains of opticians in the UK. Boots own brand products account for 75% of all sales.

Homestyle

Turnover £m

95	96	**97**
114.6	104.9	**109.4**

Operating Profit/(Loss) £m

95	96	**97**
(8.5)	(12.2)	**(11.8)**

334 total stores

102 FADS

232 Homestyle

2,402 employees

The business is a leading retailer of home decorating materials through Homestyle and FADS The Decorating Specialists.

12 The Boots Company PLC

DO IT ALL

BOOTS HEALTHCARE
INTERNATIONAL

BOOTS CONTRACT
MANUFACTURING

BOOTS PROPERTIES

Turnover £m		
95	96	97
185.3	170.7	301.4*

*100% ownership from June 1996

Turnover £m		
95	96	97
203.5	206.7	243.4

Turnover £m		
95	96	97
216.0	239.4	259.5

Turnover £m		
95	96	97
98.0	102.9	102.1

Operating Profit/(Loss) £m		
95	96	97
(6.3)	(10.1)	(6.9)*

Operating Profit/(Loss) £m		
95	96	97
9.8	(8.2)	(6.6)

Operating Profit/(Loss) £m		
95	96	97
17.8	16.7	21.2

Operating Profit/(Loss) £m		
95	96	97
66.8	68.2	72.1

171 stores

15 operating businesses
around the world

Five factories and
one major development
laboratory in the UK
and three manufacturing
businesses in Europe

936 UK properties

5,278 employees

1,836 employees

3,993 employees

89 employees

A DIY company now fully
owned by The Boots
Company

Responsible for the
development and marketing
of consumer healthcare
products in the UK, Europe,
Africa, the Indian sub-
continent, South East Asia
and Australasia. The product
range includes Strepsils,
Nurofen, Optrex, E45,
Lutsine and Onagrine.

Develops and produces a
wide range of own brand
products for Boots The
Chemists, consumer
products for Boots
Healthcare International,
and numerous products
under contract for other
companies.

Manages the group's
freehold and long leasehold
property portfolio. Its
development activities are
concentrated in the retail
sector.

13 The Boots Company PLC

APPENDIX 3 – EXPERIAN RATING OF BLUE CIRCLE INDUSTRIES PLC

 Experian LINK Business Information

Page 1

Status With Risk

Company: **Blue Circle Industries Public Limited Company**

Summary

Details

Registered Number	**00066558**
Date Incorporated	**10 June 1900**
Date Latest Accounts	**31 December 1996**
Employees	**18,538**
Sales	**£1,814.8m**
Profits	**£297.6m**
Issued Capital	**£474m**
Net Worth	**£1,211.4m**

Subject Identification

Details

Legal Form	**Public Ltd Comp (Plc)**
SIC Codes	**2410**
Previous Name	**Associated Portland Cement Manufacturers Limited (The)**
Registered Number	**00066558**
Registered Office	**84 Eccleston Square, London, SW1V 1PX**
Trading Address	**Head Office, 84 Eccleston Square, London, SW1V 1PX**
Telephone Number	**0171 828 3456**
Principal Activities	**Manufacture And Sale Of Building Materials, Cement And Home Products.**

Experian LINK Business Information

Status With Risk

Company: **Blue Circle Industries Public Limited Company**

Corporate Structure

Details

Principal Shareholders

Bulk List Of Shareholders

There are a number of entities holding shares in this company. For full details, please contact our Company Document Service on 0800 010902 which will be delighted to provide you with the information on terms as per our current price list.

Details

Subsidiaries

Blue Circle America Inc, Blue Circle Inc, Cemento Melon Sa, Ceramica Dolomite Spa, Thermopanel Ab, Compagnie Internationale Du Chautlage Sa, Blue Circle Materials Inc, Blue Circle Aggregates Inc, Circle Cement Ltd, Finimetal Sa, August Brotje Gmbh And Co KG, Malayan Cement Berhad, Armitage Shanks (South Africa) (Pty) Ltd, Wright Rain Africa (Private) Ltd

Bankers

The Royal Bank Of Scotland Plc

67 Lombard St, London, EC3P 3DL

Sort Code

15-10-00

Auditors

Ernst And Young

Directors

Current Directors

Name   **James R Loudon**

Name   **Ian S McKenzie**

Name   **Keith   Orrell-Jones**

Name   **John F Hunter**

***Experian LINK* Business Information**

Page 4

Status With Risk

Company: **Blue Circle Industries Public Limited Company**

Directors

Name   **Charles G Young**

The Old Rectory, Chipping Warden, Banbury, Oxon, OX171LR.

Name   **Sir Peter I Walters**

10, Launceston Place, London, W8 5RL.

Name   **Hugh G Beevor**

1, Saint Maur Road, London, SW6 4DR.

Company Secretary

Name   **Richard F Tapp**

33 Station Road Earls Barton Northampton NN6 0NT

Public Record Information

Details

Mortgages/Charges	**14 (Since 1/10/1984)**
Including	**Miscellaneous**
Dated	**27 April 1927**
Secured on	**£2,560,400 Debenture Stock Of The Company**
Satisfactions Recorded	**13**
Legal Notices	**None Recorded**
Total Judgments	**2**
Value	**£317**

County Court Judgments

Period	Last 12m	13-24m	25-36m	37-48m	49-60m	61-72m
Number	0	0	0	2	0	0
Value £	0	0	0	317	0	0

Search performed on 10/06/1998 at 09:53:32

02/14/00066558/98161095332Ylhy (01.05.001)

Experian LINK Business Information

Company: **Blue Circle Industries Public Limited Company**

Balance Sheet

Details

Accounts Ref. Date	**31 December**		Last Accounts	**31 December 1996**

Last Returns   **15 June 1997**

Date Of Accounts Number Of Weeks	31/12/1996 (Consol.) 52 £000	31/12/1995 (Consol.) 52 £000	31/12/1994 (Consol.) 52 £000	31/12/1993 (Consol.) 52 £000
Land And Buildings	440,000	461,100	459,400	467,200
Fixtures And Fittings	0	0	0	0
Plant And Vehicles	526,400	535,400	523,200	556,600
Total Tangible	966,400	996,500	982,600	1,023,800
Intangible	0	0	0	0
Other	231,600	193,500	187,800	182,200
Total Fixed Assets	**1,198,000**	**1,190,000**	**1,170,400**	**1,206,000**
Stocks	200,900	222,600	199,500	193,500
Work In Progress	47,200	49,100	35,700	49,200
Stocks/Work In Progress	248,100	271,700	235,200	242,700
Trade Debtors	281,500	307,600	313,700	297,200
Group Loans (Asset)	3,000	2,600	2,500	1,700
Directors Loan (Asset)	0	0	0	0
Other Debtors (Asset)	151,400	153,600	139,200	116,400
Debtors	435,900	463,800	455,400	415,300
Cash At Bank	40,900	55,800	35,100	26,600
Other Current (Asset)	503,200	567,600	475,900	360,500
Total Current Assets	**1,228,100**	**1,358,900**	**1,201,600**	**1,045,100**
Trade Creditors	132,000	139,000	131,400	124,700
Bank Overdraft	249,200	336,500	328,000	217,500
Group Loans (Liability)	500	500	500	500
Directors Loan (Liability)	0	0	0	0
Hire Purchase (Liability)	0	0	0	0
Leasing (Liability)	500	100	100	1,800
Hire Purchase/Leasing (Liability)	500	100	100	1,800
Short Loans	1,300	1,600	3,000	93,000
Corporation Tax	67,100	70,500	62,200	47,000
Dividends	66,600	62,300	58,300	51,800
Accruals/Deferred Income (Liability)	102,500	107,200	114,700	94,800
Social Security/Vat	38,100	40,400	40,300	34,800
Other Current (Liability)	55,300	57,400	49,800	43,500
Total Current Liabilities	**713,100**	**815,500**	**788,300**	**709,400**
Working Capital	**515,000**	**543,400**	**413,300**	**335,700**
Capital Employed	**1,713,000**	**1,733,400**	**1,583,700**	**1,541,700**
Group Loans (Long Term)	-	0	0	0
Director Loans (Long Term)	-	0	0	0
Hire Purchase (Long Term)	0	0	0	0
Leasing (Long Term)	600	700	600	1,800
Hire Purchase/Leasing (Long Term)	600	700	600	1,800
Other Long Term Loans	277,400	320,900	305,800	433,300

02/14/00066558/98161095332YIhy (01 05 001)

Experian LINK Business Information

Page 6

Company: **Blue Circle Industries Public Limited Company**

Date Of Accounts	31/12/1996	31/12/1995	31/12/1994	31/12/1993
Number Of Weeks	(Consol.) 52	(Consol.) 52	(Consol.) 52	(Consol.) 52
	£000	£000	£000	£000
Accruals/Deferred Income (Long Term)	5,500	2,600	6,400	6,900
Other Long Term Liabilities	102,800	85,300	71,400	31,100
Total Long Term Liabilities	386,300	409,500	384,200	473,100
Deferred Taxation	23,900	21,300	21,600	17,200
Other Provisions	91,400	127,800	65,300	70,800
Total Provisions	115,300	149,100	86,900	88,000
Total Net Assets	**1,211,400**	**1,174,800**	**1,112,600**	**980,600**
Issued Capital	471,200	473,300	471,400	453,000
Share Premium Accounts	287,700	276,000	269,200	264,800
Revaluation Reserve	37,300	40,800	44,000	46,900
Retained Earnings	247,000	224,000	171,600	135,800
Other Reserves	168,200	160,700	156,400	80,100
Total Shareholders' Funds	**1,211,400**	**1,174,800**	**1,112,600**	**980,600**

Profit and Loss

Details

Accounts Ref. Date	**31 December**		Last Accounts	**31 December 1996**

Last Returns	**15 June 1997**			

Date Of Accounts	31/12/1996	31/12/1995	31/12/1994	31/12/1993
Number Of Weeks	(Consol.) 52	(Consol.) 52	(Consol.) 52	(Consol.) 52
	£000	£000	£000	£000
Turnover (Uk)	683,400	607,300	714,400	645,900
Turnover (Export)	1,131,400	1,167,300	1,065,400	1,032,900
Total Turnover	1,814,800	1,774,600	1,779,800	1,678,800
Cost Of Sales	1,184,700	1,181,800	1,224,200	1,173,700
Total Expenses	-	-	-	-
Gross Profit	**630,100**	**592,800**	**555,600**	**505,100**
Depreciation	94,000	95,200	91,800	95,600
Other Expenses	395,400	389,800	370,400	354,800
Operating Profit	-	-	-	-
Other Income	109,900	116,700	94,200	80,400
Interest Payable	47,000	55,200	51,800	65,100
Exceptional Items	0	(700)	(43,200)	0
Discontinued Operations	0	2,400	(3,200)	0
Pre-Tax Profit/(Loss)	**297,600**	**263,800**	**184,400**	**165,600**
Tax Payable/(CR)	99,100	107,600	77,100	52,000
Extraordinary Items/(DB)	(62,100)	(4,300)	(8,100)	(5,600)
Dividends	105,900	99,900	95,800	85,900
Retained Profit/(Loss)	**30,500**	**52,000**	**3,400**	**22,100**

Experian LINK Business Information

Status With Risk

Company: **Blue Circle Industries Public Limited Company**

Salient Ratios

Details

Accounts Ref. Date	**31 December**	Last Accounts	**31 December 1996**

Last Returns **15 June 1997**

Date Of Accounts	31/12/1996	31/12/1995	31/12/1994	31/12/1993
Number Of Weeks	**52**	**52**	**52**	**52**
Salient Ratios				
Return On Capital	17.4	15.2	11.6	10.7
Profit Margin	16.4	14.9	10.4	9.9
Credit Period (Days)	57	63	64	65
Liquidity	1.7	1.7	1.5	1.5
Equity Gearing%	49.9	46.1	46.9	43.6
Debt Gearing%	22.9	27.4	27.5	44.4

Credit Evaluation

Details

Credit Opinion   **Considered equal to engagements.**

Credit Rating   **£500,000 or above**

Risk Analysis

Details

Risk Analysis   **The risk index allocated to BLUE CIRCLE INDUSTRIES PUBLIC LIMITED COMPANY is based on an analysis of the findings recorded above. In the light of the information available, the company has been found to be not only substantial in size but very sound in both trading performance and Balance Sheet strength. There is, therefore, no hesitation in awarding minimum risk status.**

Risk Score   **84 out of 100**

02/14/00066558/98161095332YIhy (01.05.001)

APPENDIX 4 – CREDIT RATING AGENCY RATING DEFINITIONS

STANDARD & POORS ISSUE CREDIT RATINGS DEFINITIONS

A Standard & Poor's issue credit rating is a current opinion of the creditworthiness of an obligor with respect to a specific financial obligation, a specific class of financial obligations, or a specific financial program (including ratings on medium-term note programs and commercial paper programs). It takes into consideration the creditworthiness of guarantors, insurers, or other forms of credit enhancement on the obligation and takes into account the currency in which the obligation is denominated. The issue credit rating is not a recommendation to purchase, sell, or hold a financial obligation, inasmuch as it does not comment as to market price or suitability for a particular investor.

Issue credit ratings are based on current information furnished by the obligors or obtained by Standard & Poor's from other sources it considers reliable. Standard & Poor's does not perform an audit in connection with any credit rating and may, on occasion, rely on unaudited financial information. Credit ratings may be changed, suspended, or withdrawn as a result of changes in, or unavailability of, such information, or based on other circumstances.

Issue credit ratings can be either long-term or short-term. Short-term ratings are generally assigned to those obligations considered short-term in the relevant market. In the US, for example, that means obligations with an original maturity of no more than 365 days – including commercial paper. Short-term ratings are also used to indicate the creditworthiness of an obligor with respect to put features on long-term obligations. The result is a dual rating, in which the short-term rating addresses the put feature, in addition to the usual long-term rating. Medium-term notes are assigned long-term ratings.

LONG-TERM ISSUE CREDIT RATINGS

Issue credit ratings are based, in varying degrees, on the following considerations:

1   Likelihood of payment-capacity and willingness of the obligor to meet its financial commitment on an obligation in accordance with the terms of the obligation.

2   Nature of and provisions of the obligation.

3   Protection afforded by, and relative position of, the obligation in the event of bankruptcy, reorganisation, or other arrangement under the laws of bankruptcy and other laws affecting creditors' rights.

The issue rating definitions are expressed in terms of default risk. As such, they pertain to senior obligations of an entity. Junior obligations are typically rated lower than senior obligations, to reflect the lower priority in bankruptcy, as noted above. (Such differentiation applies when an entity has both senior and subordinated obligations, secured and unsecured obligations, or operating company and holding company obligations.) Accordingly, in the case of junior debt, the rating may not conform exactly with the category definition.

AAA

An obligation rated AAA has the highest rating assigned by Standard & Poor's. The obligor's capacity to meet its financial commitment on the obligation is extremely strong.

AA

An obligation rated AA differs from the highest-rated obligations only in small degree. The obligor's capacity to meet its financial commitment on the obligation is very strong.

A

An obligation rated A is somewhat more susceptible to the adverse effects of changes in circumstances and economic conditions than obligations in higher-rated categories. However, the obligor's capacity to meet its financial commitment on the obligation is still strong.

BBB

An obligation rated BBB exhibits adequate protection parameters. However, adverse economic conditions or changing circumstances are more likely to lead to a weakened capacity of the obligor to meet its financial commitment on the obligation.

Obligations rated BB, B, CCC, CC, and C are regarded as having significant speculative characteristics. BB indicates the least degree of speculation and C the highest. While such obligations will likely have some quality and protective characteristics, these may be outweighed by large uncertainties or major exposures to adverse conditions.

BB

An obligation rated BB is less vulnerable to nonpayment than other speculative issues. However, it faces major ongoing uncertainties or exposure to adverse business, financial, or economic conditions which could lead to the obligor's inadequate capacity to meet its financial commitment on the obligation.

B

An obligation rated B is more vulnerable to nonpayment than obligations rated BB, but the obligor currently has the capacity to meet its financial commitment on the obligation. Adverse business, financial, or economic conditions will likely impair the obligor's capacity or willingness to meet its financial commitment on the obligation.

CCC

An obligation rated CCC is currently vulnerable to nonpayment, and is dependent upon favorable business, financial, and economic conditions for the obligor to meet its financial commitment on the obligation. In the event of adverse business, financial, or economic conditions, the obligor is not likely to have the capacity to meet its financial commitment on the obligation.

CC

An obligation rated CC is currently highly vulnerable to nonpayment.

C

The C rating may be used to cover a situation where a bankruptcy petition has been filed or similar action has been taken, but payments on this obligation are being continued.

D

An obligation rated D is in payment default. The D rating category is used when payments on an obligation are not made on the date due even if the applicable grace period has not expired, unless Standard & Poor's believes that such payments will be made during such grace period. The D rating also will be used upon the filing of a bankruptcy petition or the taking of a similar action if payments on an obligation are jeopardised.

Plus (+) or minus (–)

The ratings from AA to CCC may be modified by the addition of a plus or minus sign to show relative standing within the major rating categories.

r

This symbol is attached to the ratings of instruments with significant non-credit risks. It highlights risks to principal or volatility of expected returns, which are not addressed in the credit rating. Examples include: obligations linked or indexed to equities, currencies, or commodities; obligations exposed to severe prepayment risk – such as interest-only or principal-only mortgage securities; and obligations with unusually risky interest terms, such as inverse floaters.

MOODY'S LONG-TERM RATINGS

Debt ratings – Taxable debt and deposits globally

Aaa

Bonds which are rated Aaa are judged to be of the best quality. They carry the smallest degree of investment risk and are generally referred to as 'gilt edged.' Interest payments are protected by a large or by an exceptionally stable margin and principal is secure. While the various protective elements are likely to change, such changes as can be visualised are most unlikely to impair the fundamentally strong position of such issues.

Aa

Bonds which are rated Aa are judged to be of high quality by all standards. Together with the Aaa group they comprise what are generally known as high-grade bonds. They are rated lower than the best bonds because margins of protection may not be as large as in Aaa securities or fluctuation of protective elements may be of greater amplitude or there may be other elements present which make the long-term risk appear somewhat larger than the Aaa securities.

A

Bonds which are rated A possess many favorable investment attributes and are to be considered as upper-medium-grade obligations. Factors giving security to principal and interest are considered adequate, but elements may be present which suggest a susceptibility to impairment some time in the future.

Baa

Bonds which are rated Baa are considered as medium-grade obligations (i.e., they are neither highly protected nor poorly secured). Interest payments and principal security appear adequate for the present but certain protective elements may be lacking or may be characteristically unreliable over any great length of time. Such bonds lack outstanding investment characteristics and in fact have speculative characteristics as well.

Ba

Bonds which are rated Ba are judged to have speculative elements; their future cannot be considered as well-assured. Often the protection of interest and principal payments may be very moderate, and thereby not well safeguarded during both good and bad times over the future. Uncertainty of position characterises bonds in this class.

B

Bonds which are rated B generally lack characteristics of the desirable investment. Assurance of interest and principal payments or of maintenance of other terms of the contract over any long period of time may be small.

Caa

Bonds which are rated Caa are of poor standing. Such issues may be in default or there may be present elements of danger with respect to principal or interest.

Ca

Bonds which are rated Ca represent obligations which are speculative in a high degree. Such issues are often in default or have other marked short-comings.

C

Bonds which are rated C are the lowest rated class of bonds, and issues so rated can be regarded as having extremely poor prospects of ever attaining any real investment standing.

Moody's bond ratings, where specified, are applicable to financial contracts, senior bank obligations and insurance company senior policyholder and claims obligations with an original maturity in excess of one year. Obligations relying upon support mechanisms such as letters-of-credit and bonds of indemnity are excluded unless explicitly rated.

Obligations of a branch of a bank are considered to be domiciled in the country in which the branch is located.

Unless noted as an exception, Moody's rating on a bank's ability to repay senior obligations extends only to branches located in countries which carry a Moody's Sovereign Rating for Bank Deposits. Such branch obligations are rated at the lower of the bank's rating or Moody's Sovereign Rating for the Bank Deposits for the country in which the branch is located. When the currency in which an obligation is denominated is not the same as the currency of the country in which the obligation is domiciled, Moody's ratings do not incorporate an opinion as to whether payment of the obligation will be affected by the actions of the government controlling the currency of denomination. In addition, risk associated with bilateral conflicts between an investor's home country and either the issuer's home country or the country where an issuer branch is located are not incorporated into Moody's ratings.

Moody's makes no representation that rated bank obligations or insurance company obligations are exempt from registration under the US Securities Act of 1933 or issued in conformity with any other applicable law or regulation. Nor does Moody's represent any specific bank or insurance company obligation is legally enforceable or a valid senior obligation of a rated issuer.

Note: Moody's applies numerical modifiers 1, 2, and 3 in each generic rating classification from Aa through Caa. The modifier 1 indicates that the obligation ranks in the higher end of its generic rating category; the modifier 2 indicates a mid-range ranking; and the modifier 3 indicates a ranking in the lower end of that generic rating category.

APPENDIX 5 – BROKER'S REPORT ON BLUE CIRCLE INDUSTRIES PLC

UK BUILDING MATERIALS

Blue Circle Industries	Rating	Share price	Target price	Reuters
	3	435p	450p	**BCI.L**

Blue Circle Inds. relative to FTALLSH

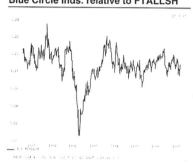

Key data	1996	1997e	1998e	1999e
Turnover	1815	2019	2143	2235
Pre-tax profit (£m)	297.6	355.5	382.0	404.5
EPS (p)	22.7	27.5	29.5	31.2
DPS (p)	13.3	14.0	14.8	15.5
Dividend Yield (%)	4.5	3.2	3.4	3.6
PE (x)	16.1	15.8	14.7	14.0
PE relative (%)	101	94	97	102
EV/EBITDA (x)	7.5	8.0	7.5	7.1
ROE (%)	9.9	11.6	11.7	11.6

Breakdown of operating profit - 1997e

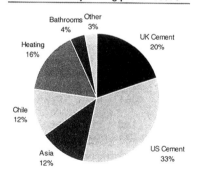

Increasingly dependable and generating wealth

1. Investment summary

The group is much better managed and more focused on generating real wealth than ever before. Quietly but surely the group is getting on with investing to improve what it already owns (e.g. cement in the UK) or acquiring to expand at sensible ratings (e.g. St Mary's Cement in Canada).

In many ways BCI is proving to be one of the most stable entities in the sector; it is not over exposed to any one market (US, UK, Europe, Chile or Malaysia, etc.) and it can often absorb the weakness of one market with the strength of another. A case in point is that cement prices in Chile are falling and profitability is being squeezed there but the group is countering this pressure with a strong drive for productivity in Chile at the same time that its UK operations are stepping up quite strongly. Cement volumes in the UK are running ahead of last year by 4% and prices are higher by a similar amount.

The core attraction of BCI is that it is stable through its attractive geographical balance, and moreover its minimal exposure to cement in Europe (by default rather than by design) has been to its advantage. **That said, these attractions are largely recognised within the share price and we thus rate the group a very sound long term hold.**

2. Business mix

The group is one of the world's leading cement producers with capacity of c25mt. It is the largest producer of cement in the UK, Denmark, Nigeria, Zimbabwe, Malaysia and Kenya. It is the second largest producer in Chile after Holderbank, about the 5th largest producer in the US and the 3rd largest producer in the Great Lakes region of Canada.

Cement accounts for 75% of group profits with the remainder being split between heating and bathrooms. There is also a small contribution from property which should grow in the early part of the coming decade as the Channel Tunnel rail link throws up development opportunities in the north east Kent corridor, especially around Ebbsfleet.

The scope for better than expected results comes from margin improvement within the European heating division as well as from better trading in its UK and Canadian cement operations. The areas of uncertainty for the group are **(i)** pricing in Chile, **(ii)** politics in Nigeria, **(iii)** the maturity of the cycle in the US, and **(iv)** the risk of overbuilding in Malaysia and of imports from Thailand.

3. Current trading

With the exception of pricing instability in Chile and a slow down in Nigeria, the group is doing well; in fact it is probably doing better than previously assumed in the US and the UK where both volumes, prices and cost efficiencies are helping to boost margins.

The bathroom division is flat whilst cost savings in the heating division are helping to boost profits in the UK. The French heating business (Celsius) is being held back by a weak economy whilst in Germany the group is benefiting from the switch over to condensation boilers as regulatory pressures encourage a switch from old technology to new, where the emissions of carbon dioxide are less.

UK BUILDING MATERIALS

With the inclusion of St Mary's we have increased our 1998/99 estimates to reflect the probable improvement in trading in Canada coupled with the likely impact of best operational practice under BCI's stewardship.

4. Wealth creation

After a decade of underperforming the sector in terms of wealth generation, the group seems not only to have learnt the script, but has begun to apply the message assertively to the business. During the 1980s into the early 1990s the group achieved a return gap (EVA) which was worse than that experienced by the sector, but over the past two years the trend has improved and over the coming 2-3 years the group is set to outpace the sector. Moreover, the group is likely to achieve a positive return gap in 1997 for the first time in over a decade, and probably the first time for almost a quarter of a century.

Wealth generation is being enhanced by a strong cycle in the US and company specific action to improve the performance of its heating assets in the UK as well as its UK cement assets beyond 1999.

Blue Circle - return gap (%)

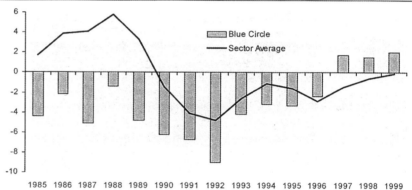

5. Strengths

As a leading cement producer the group naturally enjoys some economies of scale in terms of technological know how and buying power with regards to capital equipment, but in addition the group has number of strengths:

- market leadership in the UK, Denmark, Chile, Malaysia, and parts of Africa

- BCI is also the market leader on the East coast of the US

- an experienced and capable management team

- a group culture which is increasingly focused on wealth generation

- ongoing cash flow is strong at 10p per 100p of sales

- group is well diversified

- sanitaryware business is strong in both the UK and Italy

- better results are increasing the strategic value of the heating division

- the group has demonstrated a rigorous control of its costs; and

- surplus land assets are estimated to be worth £250m

6. Weaknesses

The single biggest weakness of the group is that the shares are not as cheap as some others in the sector and therefore, although the company specifics are compelling, the valuation is a touch rich. That said there are a few weaknesses within BCI. The group:

- does not control all of the cash flow from its associates which represent up to 25% of group profits

- is exposed to the over priced Chilean cement market

- faces uncertainty over the business cycle in the US

- is exposed to the medium term threat of too much capacity coming on stream in Malaysia; and

- faces the threat of Thai imports into Malaysia due to the marked de-valuation of the baht

6. Valuation

The group is not under valued. Its attractions are generally recognised by the market. We estimate that its strategic value is c.410p per share which compares with a market price of 435p. In addition we note that the group is reasonably fully priced residing on:

- a sales multiple of 1.90x with operating margins of 15%. This compares with a heavyside average sales multiple of 1.0x off operating margins of 9.7%. On a pro-rata bases, BCI should be on a sales multiple of 1.5-1.6x , not necessarily 1.9x.

- high PBIT and PBDIT multiples of 10.2x and 8.0x, respectively, although its superior RoI merits this to some extent.

- A PER of 15x for 1998 is not especially attractive.

Operationally the group is attractive; but unless the group does considerably better than assumed, it is difficult to argue that the shares are under valued. A large amount of its attractions are recognised.

Schroders

UK BUILDING MATERIALS

Blue Circle Industries plc - Profit and loss account (1990-1999e)

Year ended 31 December	1990	1991	1992	1993	1994	1995	H1 96	1996	H1 97e	1997e	1998e	1999e
Turnover breakdown:												
Cement - UK	389.4	320.0	275.3	274.3	317.7	317.5	153.6	311.6	164.5	333.8	357.5	375.6
- Europe	0.0	0.0	52.5	49.1	51.6	54.5	25.4	55.4	26.6	58.0	60.0	62.5
- USA	244.4	219.0	226.1	311.7	348.1	380.5	203.7	418.4	203.6	418.3	441.8	450.6
- Canada									40.0	117.8	138.6	147.0
- Chile	47.5	57.0	80.1	109.1	114.9	145.2	80.4	162.0	85.4	172.0	182.5	191.6
- Africa	14.4	20.3	19.1	20.6	23.1	24.6	10.6	16.6	12.8	20.0	24.0	28.0
- Asia	0.5	0.7	1.1	1.2	1.7	2.5	0.9	2.5	0.9	2.5	2.5	2.5
- Other and bricks	0.0	2.8	32.6	60.7	19.3	4.0	1.5	0.0	0.0	0.0	0.0	0.0
Total Heavy Building Materials	**696.2**	**619.8**	**686.8**	**826.7**	**876.4**	**928.8**	**476.1**	**966.5**	**533.8**	**1,122.4**	**1,206.9**	**1,257.9**
UK - Heating	187.4	188.0	184.4	196.7	193.4	184.0	95.1	197.0	100.3	207.8	217.2	228.0
- Bathrooms	116.2	104.4	100.3	98.9	104.1	106.3	54.4	108.0	64.7	128.5	134.9	140.3
- Domestic appliances	55.1	47.5	48.2	37.0	20.1	0.0	0.0	0.0	0.0	0.0	0.0	0.0
- Other	3.7	35.6	39.3	0.0	0.0	5.8	0.0	3.3	0.0	0.0	0.0	0.0
Thermopanel	-	-	27.4	24.4	26.4	26.6	14.0	30.4	15.2	33.0	35.0	37.0
Ceramica Dolomite	15.6	46.7	50.4	51.6	56.0	60.4	35.3	63.9	38.1	69.0	72.0	76.5
Celsius	-	-	95.5	190.4	191.9	191.8	84.9	188.3	97.8	217.0	225.7	232.5
Brotje	-	-	112.3	222.5	231.7	252.5	109.8	224.5	102.5	209.6	219.0	230.0
Total Home Products	**378.0**	**422.2**	**657.8**	**821.5**	**823.6**	**827.4**	**393.5**	**815.5**	**418.7**	**864.9**	**903.8**	**944.3**
Property	28.9	39.9	19.4	24.1	72.3	17.0	1.9	30.8	1.9	30.0	30.0	30.0
Other	111.6	67.5	6.1	6.5	7.5	1.4	2.2	2.0	2.0	2.0	2.5	3.0
Total sales	**1,214.7**	**1,149.4**	**1,370.1**	**1,678.8**	**1,779.8**	**1,774.6**	**873.7**	**1,814.8**	**956.3**	**2,019.3**	**2,143.2**	**2,235.2**
Less associate sales	**0.0**	**0.0**	**0.0**	**0.0**	**0.0**	**0.0**	**0.0**	**0.0**	**0.0**	**0.0**	**0.0**	**0.0**
Group sales	**1,214.7**	**1,149.4**	**1,370.1**	**1,678.8**	**1,779.8**	**1,774.6**	**873.7**	**1,814.8**	**956.3**	**2,019.3**	**2,143.2**	**2,235.2**
Operating profit breakdown:												
Cement - UK	68.1	40.9	24.3	36.1	64.1	65.3	24.0	59.4	28.7	71.0	79.4	85.4
- Europe	0.9	2.5	4.3	3.1	3.1	6.1	2.8	7.1	3.0	7.5	8.5	9.0
- USA	18.4	11.5	13.6	32.6	48.6	63.5	25.1	75.3	27.5	82.6	86.5	87.0
- Canada									8.5	36.5	38.6	41.6
- Chile	12.8	14.8	22.5	34.5	35.4	45.5	20.5	43.1	20.2	43.0	45.0	49.0
- Africa	19.2	17.7	10.3	13.0	24.0	25.0	10.8	19.0	11.4	20.0	21.5	23.5
- Marine cement	2.0	2.7	4.3	4.9	5.4	5.5	2.0	5.5	2.2	6.0	6.5	7.0
- Asia	12.0	16.0	18.4	20.4	20.3	27.8	17.8	38.0	19.9	42.5	49.0	53.0
UK - Bricks	3.5	0.6	0.1	0.2	0.8	1.6	0.0	(0.1)	0.0	0.5	1.0	1.5
UK - Waste	-	-	(1.0)	(8.3)	(6.5)	(0.5)	0.1	(0.2)	0.1	0.2	0.8	1.0
Other	(5.9)	0.0	-	1.2	1.6	1.7	(0.8)	(2.8)	0.3	1.0	1.0	1.0
Total Heavy Building Materials	**131.0**	**106.7**	**96.8**	**137.7**	**196.8**	**241.5**	**102.3**	**244.3**	**121.7**	**310.8**	**337.7**	**359.0**
UK - Heating	20.3	22.6	23.5	26.5	21.5	11.6	10.1	19.1	14.0	26.5	30.0	32.0
- Bathrooms	17.4	14.1	11.8	8.8	11.8	12.8	6.1	12.9	7.1	15.0	17.0	18.0
- Domestic appliances	(2.6)	(1.0)	(0.8)	(2.2)	0.0	0.0	0.0	0.0	0.0	0.0	0.0	0.0
- Other	4.6	6.4	0.3	0.2	1.3	(1.0)	0.4	(1.5)	0.0	0.0	0.0	0.0
Thermopanel	-	-	2.1	3.3	3.6	2.2	0.7	3.7	0.8	4.0	4.5	5.0
Ceramica Dolomite	3.2	9.4	11.1	11.3	12.8	13.3	6.6	11.7	6.2	11.0	12.0	13.5
Celsius	-	-	8.7	10.1	12.8	4.1	2.4	11.2	2.6	12.1	13.8	15.2
Brotje	-	-	3.5	6.4	4.0	1.1	(4.5)	2.5	1.5	5.0	5.4	6.1
Total Home Products	**42.9**	**51.5**	**60.2**	**64.4**	**67.8**	**44.1**	**21.8**	**59.6**	**32.2**	**73.6**	**82.7**	**89.8**
Property	15.3	11.6	(13.6)	4.8	11.0	3.3	1.9	11.9	1.2	3.0	3.0	3.0
Other	6.9	(6.3)	(12.0)	(8.5)	(10.9)	(2.6)	(4.5)	(10.9)	(5.4)	(11.0)	(11.2)	(11.5)
Total operating profits	**196.1**	**163.5**	**131.4**	**198.4**	**264.7**	**286.3**	**121.5**	**304.9**	**149.7**	**376.3**	**412.2**	**440.3**
Net interest	(1.1)	(22.8)	(25.8)	(32.8)	(20.9)	(13.5)	(5.2)	(7.3)	(6.5)	(20.8)	(30.2)	(35.8)
Exceptionals	(25.0)	(42.1)	(11.8)	0.0	(59.4)	(9.0)	0.0	0.0	0.0	0.0	0.0	(25.0)
Profit before tax - FRS3	**170.0**	**98.6**	**93.8**	**165.6**	**184.4**	**263.8**	**116.3**	**297.6**	**143.2**	**355.5**	**382.0**	**379.5**
Profit before tax - Normalised	**195.0**	**140.7**	**105.6**	**165.6**	**243.8**	**272.8**	**116.3**	**297.6**	**143.2**	**355.5**	**382.0**	**404.5**
Tax	(42.0)	(35.9)	(53.1)	(52.0)	(77.1)	(107.6)	(39.3)	(99.1)	(46.5)	(115.5)	(123.2)	(122.4)
Preference dividends	(8.3)	(8.2)	(8.2)	(8.2)	(8.2)	(8.2)	(4.1)	(7.9)	(4.0)	(7.9)	(7.9)	(7.9)
Minorities	(3.8)	(4.7)	(6.5)	(5.6)	(8.1)	(13.7)	(7.4)	(17.7)	(8.3)	(19.8)	(22.8)	(24.7)
Profit after tax and minorities	**115.9**	**49.8**	**26.0**	**99.8**	**91.0**	**134.3**	**65.5**	**172.9**	**84.4**	**212.3**	**228.1**	**224.5**
Dividends	(62.9)	(62.0)	(76.4)	(77.7)	(87.6)	(91.7)	(31.2)	(98.0)	(33.3)	(103.5)	(109.1)	(114.6)
Retained profit	**53.0**	**(12.2)**	**(50.4)**	**22.1**	**3.4**	**42.6**	**34.3**	**74.9**	**51.1**	**108.7**	**119.0**	**109.9**
EPS (p) - FRS3 Diluted	18.1	7.3	3.6	14.6	20.1	18.1	9.4	22.7	11.7	27.5	29.5	29.1
EPS (p) - FRS3	**21.3**	**8.6**	**4.0**	**14.5**	**12.7**	**18.4**	**8.9**	**23.5**	**11.4**	**28.7**	**30.8**	**30.4**
EPS (p) - Normalised	24.8	13.3	4.8	14.5	21.1	21.4	8.9	23.5	11.4	28.7	30.8	32.7
EPS (p) - Norm. & Diluted	**21.0**	**11.2**	**4.3**	**14.6**	**17.0**	**18.7**	**9.4**	**22.7**	**11.7**	**27.5**	**29.5**	**31.2**
EPS Growth (%)	(10.2%)	(46.5%)	(61.4%)	235.7%	16.6%	10.2%	16.8%	21.4%	24.4%	21.2%	7.1%	5.6%
Group operating margin (%)	**16.1%**	**14.2%**	**9.6%**	**11.8%**	**14.9%**	**16.1%**	**13.9%**	**16.8%**	**15.6%**	**18.6%**	**19.2%**	**19.7%**

UK BUILDING MATERIALS

Blue Circle Industries plc - Cashflow (1992-1999e)

Year ended 31 December	1992	1993	1994	1995	H1 96	1996	H1 97e	1997e
Pre tax profits	93.8	165.6	184.4	263.8	116.3	297.6	143.2	355.5
Depreciation	94.3	95.6	91.8	95.2	48.5	94.0	50.0	105.0
Exceptionals	0.0	0.0	0.0	0.0	0.0	(40.4)	0.0	0.0
Associates	(27.1)	(18.1)	(31.7)	(33.7)	(31.5)	(40.1)	(34.7)	(44.1)
Profits from asset sales and timing differences	(21.6)	(31.8)	20.5	(11.5)	(14.0)	3.4	(5.0)	(10.0)
Funds from operations	139.4	211.3	265.0	313.8	119.3	314.5	153.5	406.4
Share issues	244.5	6.8	91.3	6.3	5.0	6.0	0.0	0.0
Asset disposals	9.0	14.7	41.3	20.8	4.2	22.4	0.0	0.0
Other disposals	106.1	0.8	16.5	66.8	19.0	17.2	0.0	0.0
Total funds generated	499.0	233.6	414.1	407.7	147.5	360.1	153.5	406.4
Dividends	75.2	82.8	82.4	93.4	(2.2)	102.0	40.1	108.0
Taxation	36.8	33.1	38.3	71.9	24.2	72.7	39.3	99.1
Stock	(15.4)	(30.1)	3.9	27.5	10.3	(1.6)	23.8	32.8
Debtors	11.4	18.4	22.8	(17.7)	50.1	13.2	8.2	16.6
Creditors	14.1	4.6	(53.0)	(3.0)	5.0	(25.8)	(6.7)	(16.4)
Operational outflows	122.1	108.8	94.4	172.1	87.4	160.5	104.6	240.1
Asset purchases	88.0	82.0	97.5	124.1	54.7	153.0	115.0	245.0
Investments	5.5	0.0	0.0	0.0	1.8	5.0	0.0	0.0
Acquisitions	216.5	0.0	1.1	6.2	1.7	37.0	235.0	235.0
Other including foreign exchange	75.1	(1.4)	(12.7)	15.2	(5.5)	(30.6)	0.0	0.0
Total cash outflow	507.2	189.4	180.3	317.6	140.1	324.9	454.6	720.1
Net cash (out) / inflow	(8.2)	44.2	233.8	90.1	7.4	35.2	(301.1)	(313.7)
Net (debt)/ cash (year end)	(404.5)	(360.3)	(126.5)	(36.4)	(29.0)	(1.2)	(302.3)	(314.9)
Ordinary shareholders' funds	856.1	873.5	1,005.5	1,068.0	1,101.4	1,109.9	1,161.0	1,218.6
Ordinary and preference shareholders' funds	963.3	980.6	1,112.6	1,174.8	1,208.2	1,211.4	1,262.5	1,320.1
Gearing net	42.0%	36.7%	11.4%	3.1%	2.4%	0.1%	23.9%	23.9%
Interest cover (x)	4.6	6.0	9.8	20.5	23.4	41.8	23.0	18.1

Blue Circle Industries plc - Valuation matrix

Valuation Matrix	1990	1991	1992	1993	1994	1995	1996	1997e
Ordinary share price (p)	215.7	237.6	207.2	261.2	312.5	301.3	365.8	435.0
Preference share price (p)	119.5	130.3	123.9	150.8	166.7	157.3	190.2	226.0
No. of ordinary shares	572.6	580.9	687.2	691.8	728.6	733.0	739.4	739.5
No. of preference shares	107.6	107.3	107.2	107.1	107.1	107.1	107.1	107.1
Equity market value (£'m)	1363.4	1520.3	1556.5	1968.2	2455.7	2377.3	2908.5	3458.9
Minorities (£'m)	28.4	32.2	45.3	46.9	52.2	60.6	63.9	69.8
Net debt/ (cash) (£'m)	352.1	396.3	404.5	360.3	126.5	36.4	1.2	314.9
Total value (£'m)	1743.9	1948.8	2006.3	2375.4	2634.4	2474.3	2973.6	3843.6
Sales multiple (x)	1.44	1.70	1.46	1.41	1.48	1.39	1.64	1.90
Operating margin (%)	13.0%	10.6%	6.8%	9.4%	11.9%	12.6%	13.2%	15.0%
PBIT multiple (x)	8.89	11.92	15.27	11.97	9.95	8.64	9.75	10.21
PBDIT multiple (x)	6.36	8.05	8.89	8.08	7.39	6.49	7.45	7.99
NAV (p)	126.4	121.0	124.6	126.3	138.0	145.7	150.1	164.8
NAV - adding back goodwill (p)	228.6	224.5	224.3	225.3	227.0	234.2	238.4	256.0
NAV multiple (x)	1.71	1.96	1.66	2.07	2.26	2.07	2.44	2.64
NAV multiple (x) - adding back goodwill	0.94	1.06	0.92	1.16	1.38	1.29	1.53	1.70
PER (x)	10.3	21.1	47.7	17.9	18.4	16.1	16.1	15.8
Yield (%)	6.7%	6.1%	7.2%	5.4%	4.7%	5.2%	4.5%	3.2%
Dividend Cover (x)	2.3	1.2	0.4	1.3	1.8	1.7	1.8	2.1
RoE (%)	10.2%	5.2%	2.4%	6.4%	8.1%	8.3%	9.9%	11.6%
ROI (%)	10.9%	8.9%	6.3%	9.6%	13.6%	14.9%	15.8%	15.8%

REFERENCES

Copeland, T., Koller, T. and Murrin, J. (1996) *Valuation: measuring and managing the value of companies*, (2nd edn), New York, McKinsey & Company, Inc., John Wiley & sons, Inc.

King, M. (1997), a lecture at the London School of Economics, 'The Inflation Target Five Years On', 29th October.

Organisation for Economic Co-operation and Development (1997) *OECD Economic Outlook*, 62, December.

Porter, M.E. (1996) 'What is strategy?', *Harvard Business Review*, November–December.

Sloan, R.G. (1996) 'Using earnings and free cash flow to evaluate corporate performance', *Journal of Applied Corporate Finance*, Vol. 9, No. 1.

ACKNOWLEDGEMENTS

Grateful acknowledgement is made to the following sources for permission to reproduce material in this unit:

Text

Blue Circle Industries plc for permission to use extracts from their *1997/98 Annual Report and Accounts*; The Boots Company plc for permission to use extracts from their *1997 Annual Report*; *Box 7.2:* Luce, E. (1998) 'Credit agency admits it failed to predict Asia woes', *Financial Times*, 14 January 1998; Box 6.1 and Appendix 3: Courtesy of Experian Ltd; Appendix 4 (Part A): Extract from the Standard and Poor's Ratings Services Web Site: www.ratings.standardpoor.com, courtesy of Standard and Poor's; Appendix 4 (Part B): Extract from Moody's Investors Service Web Site: www.moodys.com/index.shtml, courtesy of Moody's Investors Service; Appendix 5: Extract from Broker's Report on Blue Circle Industries plc, courtesy of Schroder Securities Limited.

Cartoons

p. 5: © Mark Litzler; p. 10: © 1997 Roger Beale; p. 14: © Ed Fisher; p. 18: © Roger Beale from the *Financial Times*; p. 31 © 1998 Leo Cullum.

B821 FINANCIAL STRATEGY